**The Decline of
American Political Parties
1952–1980**

The Decline of
American Political Parties
1952–1980

Martin P. Wattenberg

Harvard University Press
Cambridge, Massachusetts, and London, England   1984

Library of Congress Cataloging in Publication Data

Wattenberg, Martin P., 1956–
The decline of American political parties, 1952–1980.

Bibliography: p.
Includes index.
1. Political parties—United States.
2. United States—Politics and government—1945–   .
I. Title.
JK2261.W37   1984   324.273   83-12683
ISBN 0-674-19430-6 (alk. paper)

For my parents

Contents

Foreword

by Walter Dean Burnham

The history of American electoral politics is filled with many kinds of change. We need only think, for example, of the apparently cyclical changes associated with critical realignments, or of such short-term events as the "deviating elections" identified by the Michigan Survey Research Center/CPS group. But there are certain momentous sea changes that go far beyond these in their implications for the organization of democracy in America. The prime characteristics of such sea changes are that they involve the creation (or dissipation) of key institutional structures of political action, that they evolve over a considerable period of time, and that they produce an ordering of politics that lasts an extremely long time.

One good example of such a change was the creation of the modern party system as organizer of a national electoral market in the 1820s and 1830s. This most complex sequence of events and political choices, about which a true mountain of historians' research now exists, rightly goes under such names as "the democratic revolution" or "the Jacksonian revolution." For it involved a thoroughgoing recasting of American politics from its constitutional foundations upward and led to a golden age of party politics that lasted for the rest of the nineteenth century.

An equally good example of sea change, it seems to me, forms the subject of this impressive survey by Martin P. Wattenberg—the rapid decline of American political parties over the past generation, from the levels of revitalized activity and effectiveness they had achieved in and just after the New Deal period. More precisely, the subject of Wattenberg's penetrating scrutiny is change in the behavioral, attitudinal, and cognitive links between individual voters and the objects of their political choice, or what Frank Sorauf has described as "party-in-the-electorate." The tradeoff among these objects is, as it has always been, between parties and individual candidates.

Wattenberg's analysis makes important aspects of the party-decline problem very clear. For one thing, it abundantly confirms that the balance between party and candidate as cognitive objects has swung overwhelmingly toward candidate imagery over the generation extending from 1952 to 1980. Equally, the analysis in this volume includes one of the few rigorously conducted studies of change in media orientation and coverage during election campaigns now in existence, and evaluates as well the growth of PACs and other non-party financing vehicles and their implications for structuring electoral campaigns and images. The author places considerable stress on the importance of the rules changes—the presidential-nomination reforms of the early 1970s—in conducing to candidate-dominated elections; though his own data make it very clear that the decline in the affective relevance of parties to voter decision was well under way before Messrs. McGovern and Fraser did their work.

One of the more important findings of this study, not so frequently mentioned by authors of the "party's over" school, is that this decline has significant limits. Thus, the survey data do not lend themselves well to an argument that the decline is the fruit of growing hostility, rejection, or active "alienation" on the part of the electorate. Something more subtle—and perhaps more pernicious—is involved: a fadeout of party generally, with responses shifting especially strongly over the years from positive-negative (like Democrats and dislike Republicans, or vice versa) toward neutral-neutral (indifferent to both). At the same time, Wattenberg is almost certainly right to stress that this movement is an incomplete trend toward something, and that that something (zero partisanship) has not remotely been reached yet. What is involved is not a dichotomy—once party, now no party—but a continuum, a process. Wattenberg is also on firm ground when he insists that the overwhelming bulk of this process is to be accounted for on political rather than on sociodemographic grounds such as generational replacement or increasing education levels.

One of the immense benefits accruing to scholarship from studying this particular sea change is that most of it has occurred since the inauguration of the first nationwide scientific surveys in 1952. With a full generation of such surveys behind us, students of American voting behavior are now beginning to possess adequate time series that give us a much better sense of change and continuity at or near the individual level than we have ever had before. To be sure, I am not of the school which believes that an ounce of survey data is worth a ton of contextualist, aggregate, or other information. But as we all know, it matters immensely to our understanding that we have this survey-based time series. Wattenberg has given us a solid, penetrating look at the terrain. He includes not only an inventory of covariations over time, but sets clear limits to the scope of the change toward decline in the "party-in-the-electorate."

In this regard, one is particularly struck by the isomorphism of the major changes that are the subject of this work. They not only covary over time, they appear to reinforce each other. As the salience of party-in-the-electorate decays, the media coverage of elections shifts heavily from many references to party toward preoccupations with candidates—one is tempted to say, American politics as understood and reported by *People* magazine. While affective change toward parties seems to take the form of neutralization rather than outright hostility, this would hardly be inconsistent with the view that the reformers of 1971–72 were impelled to make changes restoring the legitimacy of the convention institution and challenging the power of party leaders. Under the circumstances as described here, these changes inevitably reinforced candidate salience as it undercut party salience. "Voting the man rather than the party" now appears to have acquired a real place in the American political culture's pantheon, as the author's data duly reveal. Meanwhile, candidates—and their operatives, their associated PACs, and other financiers—have every incentive to organize their campaigns and what they do in office so as to encourage nonpartisanship. And, while it is true that generational replacement is no adequate explanation for what has been occurring, it is also true that the younger and "newer" the age cohort is, the more extreme is the tendency toward zero partisanship described in these pages. All of these characteristics, taken together, would give us little reason to assume that the sea change of 1952–1980 is likely to be dramatically reversed any time soon unless (as happened around 1932) some overwhelming politico-economic catastrophe hits the system, and moreover hits it in a party-redefining way.

Well, who cares? What difference does it make? From V. O. Key, Jr., to Giovanni Sartori, serious theorists of party and its necessary link to democracy have stressed the vital importance of party again and again. When parties are absent or, as in the world described by the author of this work, have become Cheshire cats of which very little is left but the smile, pathologies multiply. As Key classically demonstrated in his magisterial *Southern Politics in State and Nation* (1949), pure candidate-domination of elections is a recipe for irresponsible, unaccountable performance in office, and is equally a recipe for domination of the political order by the haves at the expense of the have-nots. This candidate-domination, while preserving the forms of democracy, negates its substance. Sartori's analysis in *Parties and Party Systems* (1976) addressed the problem from the top down: "No parties at all leaves a society out of reach, out of control, and no modernized regime can afford, in the long run, to settle on this unsafe and unproductive solution." In other words, elites cannot govern without them. The point is still more obvious in the United States than elsewhere, since the founding fathers bequeathed us a Constitution ingeniously designed to fragment political power and frustrate the creation of any government at all, as that term is commonly understood in other democracies. It has been driven home for the more remote historical past by two seminal discussions by leading historians—James Sterling Young, writing in 1966 on politics in Washington before the first of our sea changes (*The Washington Community, 1800–1828*); and Eric McKitrick, writing in his article "Party Politics and the Union and Confederate War Efforts" (1967) on the Confederacy's lack of parties as a prime contributor to its destruction in the Civil War. The point is of course central to recent literature on Congress's "electoral connection" in an age of party decline.

Wattenberg's book performs an important service to scholarship and to the interested public outside the groves of academe. He spells out many of the most important components of the problem of decline in party-in-the-electorate, but he does so with admirable clarity and concision. The data are there, but they are presented in ways that are usually understandable to readers not versed in the higher methodological arcana of political research. The author is circumspect in his conclusions, not venturing as far from the shores of his evidence as I might. But they are powerful nonetheless, as benefits the vital importance of the subject that this book illuminates.

Massachusetts Institute of Technology
Cambridge, Massachusetts

Preface

This book goes to press during an election year that may well prove to be a crucial turning point for the future of American political parties. For nearly three decades the American public has been drifting away from the two major parties. Once the central guiding forces in American electoral behavior, the parties are now perceived with almost complete indifference by a large proportion of the population. The decline of public affection for the parties has not been due to any greater negative feelings about the Democrats and Republicans but rather to an increasing sense that the parties just no longer matter much in the governmental process. For example, in 1980 a representative sample of the population was asked four separate open-ended questions about their feelings toward the major parties—what they liked about each and disliked about each. Over a third of those interviewed responded identically to all four questions, saying that they had neither any likes nor any dislikes about the Democrats or the Republicans! When these same questions were first asked in the 1952 election study, only 10 percent of the sample responded in this way. At that time, such indifference usually proved to be part of a more general sense of political apathy and lack of political knowledge; today it is much more likely to be a specific indicator of apathy and lack of knowledge about the parties themselves. The small percentage who were neutral toward both parties in the 1950s were largely politically inactive and hence inconsequential in the voting process; today this significantly larger group plays a critical swing role in elections and is responsible for the much discussed increase in the volatility of American electoral behavior.

It would perhaps be better for the parties if the public had become more negative rather than more neutral toward them. Negative attitudes could easily be turned into positive attitudes by better performance or a change in policies. To make people care about political parties once again may well be more difficult. As argued in this book, it is increasingly difficult for Americans to see the relevance of political parties in this candidate-centered age of mass media.

Nevertheless, it is not inconceivable that the decline of political parties could begin to reverse in the near future. Another theme of this book is that the public responds to how political events are presented to them, and since the Reagan administration took office the prospects for party revitalization have definitely improved. What Reagan has accomplished thus far has been done with more unified party support than had been seen in Washington in decades. On the two key votes of 1981, for example, on the tax cut and the budget resolution, Reagan held all but one Republican vote in the House. On the other side, the Democrats have been forced into a much more unified stance than usual, much like Western settlers forming a circle to protect themselves. Differences concerning what the Democratic Party is for continue to be wide, but Reagan has given party members a clear sense of what they are against.

Thus, by 1982 conditions were ripe for some strengthening of partisanship in the electorate, which in fact occurred. Identification with the parties increased from 68 percent in 1980 to 72 percent in 1982, and the percentage of voters casting a party-line vote rose to its highest level since 1970 for both House and Senate contests. Ticket-splitting was also down, with only 24 percent voting for different parties for House and Senate compared to 31 percent in 1980. Most important, the public image of the parties showed signs of strengthening. Only 28.5 percent of those interviewed in 1982 expressed a neutral attitude toward both parties, compared to 36.5 percent in 1980—a particularly striking finding if one considers the lower degree of political stimulus involved in congressional elections.

Yet it is still far too early to say that partisanship is on the road to recovery. It remains to be seen whether partisan feelings can be rekindled in the midst of the hoopla of a presidential campaign when the candidates will undoubtedly receive the bulk of media attention. Even if the candidates act more as partisans than in the past, will a public accustomed to voting the man and not the party perceive the linkage between party and candidate? The answer will be of prime importance to the future of American political parties.

Acknowledgments

When I first became interested in survey research some years ago, what most fascinated me was that often I would find my preconceived notions contradicted by the data. Any doubts as to whether social science was really worthwhile were dispelled as I came to realize how one could more fully understand politics with the aid of survey data.

This book represents one such case where my initial ideas failed to match the empirical evidence. If I appear to devote too much space in the text to discounting particular explanations for the decline of partisanship, it is because at first these seemed quite plausible to me. Originally, I started out to do a modest term paper for Samuel Eldersveld's political parties seminar on why people had become negative toward parties. Finding that neutral rather than negative attitudes had increased most, I began to develop a new theoretical perspective that fit better with my initial findings, and which eventually led me to investigate other pieces of available data on the subject.

As this work proceeded I was fortunate to have parts of it accepted for publication. A revised version of the original term paper was published under the title "The Decline of Political Partisanship in the United States: Negativity or Neutrality?" in the *American Political Science Review* (vol. 75 [1981]: 941–950) and has been adapted here in parts of Chapters 4 and 5. One segment of Chapter 4 was also taken from a piece on realignment by Arthur Miller and me, "Decay in Regional Party Coalitions: 1952–1980," written for Seymour Martin Lipset's *Party Coalitions in the 1980s* (San Francisco: Institute for Contemporary Studies, pp. 341–370). Chapter 6 is an extended version of an article that appeared as "From Parties to Candidates: Examining the Role of the Media" in the *Public Opinion Quarterly* (vol. 46 [1982]: 216–227). And Chapter 3 has been adapted from another co-authored article with Arthur Miller, "Measuring Party Identification: Independent or No Partisan Preference?" which appeared in the

American Journal of Political Science (vol. 27 [1983]: 106–121). I benefited a great deal from the comments of anonymous journal reviewers and from editorial work on the text by several editors. In particular, I owe a special debt of gratitude to my editors at Harvard University Press, Aida Donald and Katarina Rice.

Thanks are due to graduate school advisers at Michigan and to my friends at the Center for Political Studies for making the Center such a stimulating place to do electoral research. My advisers each deserve a special note of thanks. As my academic adviser, Warren Miller offered both major substantive and editorial advice throughout. His detailed critique of my first draft was especially valuable in helping me organize the chapters more coherently and in further drawing out the implications of my findings. Philip Converse profoundly influenced my thinking at several points in this work by his many writings on the topic, and I benefited greatly from his counsel on numerous methodological and substantive questions. I am also greatly indebted to Samuel Eldersveld, who was instrumental in getting me started on this topic and in convincing me that I was on to something worth pursuing. Last but not least, Arthur Miller—teacher, co-author, and close friend—provided the most constant source of day-to-day guidance as I wrote this book. His influence on the ideas expressed in this book have been pervasive. Needless to say, he and all others should be given only credit for what is written here, as the responsibility for any blame remains purely my own.

Newport Beach, California

**The Decline of
American Political Parties
1952–1980**

Introduction

Political parties have been accorded a preeminent position in the study of American politics. For nearly a century political scientists have written of the potential of political parties to establish effective popular control over the government. In a system designed to fragment political power, parties have been held to be the one institution capable of providing a unifying centripetal force. The functions that parties have been said to perform in American society are impressive and diverse. These include:

1. Generating symbols of identification and loyalty.
2. Aggregating and articulating political interests.
3. Mobilizing majorities in the electorate and in government.
4. Socializing voters and maintaining a popular following.
5. Organizing dissent and opposition.
6. Recruiting political leadership and seeking governmental offices.
7. Institutionalizing, channeling, and socializing conflict.

8. Overriding the dangers of sectionalism and promoting the national interest.
9. Implementing policy objectives.
10. Legitimizing decisions of government.
11. Fostering stability in government.

Given all of these functions, many political scientists have accepted E. E. Schattschneider's famous assertion that modern democracy is unthinkable save in terms of parties.[1] Not surprisingly, then, the various indications that political parties have weakened in recent years have been met with a great deal of alarm among commentators on American politics. David Broder, for example, has stated flatly, "The governmental system is not working because the political parties are not working."[2] Although most experts would not go so far, few would deny that the decline of American political parties has had a significant impact on the character of politics in this country.

Perhaps the most frequently cited consequences of the decline of parties are the growing importance of special interest groups and the dwindling of the principles of collective responsibility. The result, as Morris Fiorina has written, is that we now have "a system that articulates interests superbly but aggregates them poorly."[3] The making of public policy has thus become a more conflictual process with far less central direction and coherence. Individual policy decisions are increasingly made by ad hoc coalitions without relation to other policies. As Jimmy Carter found out during his four years in office, governing without the continuous support of a political party is an extremely difficult task.

Yet the question of party decline is a complex one, for political parties are complex, multifaceted institutions.

While most of the attention has been focused on the aspects of parties that have been weakened, there is evidence suggesting that in certain aspects parties have been strengthened. According to Malcolm Jewell and David Olson, for example, state political party organizations have been revitalized with the result being a more active role for state parties.[4] And on the national level, Cornelius Cotter and John Bibby have concluded from their extensive study of the history of national party organizations that there has been a growth in terms of institutionalization and nationalization of the parties in recent years.[5]

Thus, although most of the evidence does point toward party decline, to make global statements about the decay, decomposition, disappearance, or end of parties (as many have) may lead us to overlook the aspects of parties that have not been weakened. In order to get beyond the "sky-is-falling" stage in the discussion of parties, it must be recognized that not all the trends match and that evidence about one particular aspect is not necessarily generalizable to the condition of parties as a whole. As Austin Ranney has noted, those who have written about changes in the strength of parties all have something in mind, but the "something" differs from one observer to another.[6]

Political scientists who write about political parties fall into two main types, according to the noted British author S. E. Finer—"those who think of parties as things that *do*, and those who think of them as things that *are*."[7] The former primarily concern themselves with how well parties as organizations perform functions related to the machinery of government and the contesting of elections. Those among this school who are most empirically oriented study party activists and what they do; others study the various structures of the parties and how they operate. In contrast, writers who concern themselves with what parties *are* focus mainly on partisan attitudes among the mass public. Authors of this school address questions of alignment and dealignment in the party system, largely based on micro-level survey data on party identification and voting patterns.

This book clearly belongs in the latter category, but what political parties *do* has in fact been a prime motivating factor. If it were not for the crucial role that parties play in the operation of American government, the study of partisanship in the electorate would be far less important. Furthermore, one can reasonably infer that what parties are from the perspective of the mass electorate will have a major impact on what parties do in the political system. For example, if members of the electorate cast their ballots on the basis of factors other than partisanship, then those public officials who are elected can be expected to act more as individuals and less as members of a collective body committed to common goals. Similarly, if the mass public conceptualizes issues in terms of candidates rather than in terms of parties, then the direction of public policy can be expected to be hardly any more stable than the names on the ballot from year to year.

Of course, the flow of causality is by no means a unidirectional one from the state of parties in the electorate to the state of parties in government. If parties in government are weakened, the public will naturally have less of a stimulus to think of themselves politically in partisan terms. In fact, it will be argued here that one of the major factors behind the decline of partisanship in the electorate is that parties have become less integral in the processes of governing and campaigning, thereby resulting in the mass public's more neutral attitudes toward them. However, these altered public attitudes have themselves become a major reason why it will be very difficult to go back and reinstitutionalize political parties. Political behavior has a distinct habitual flavor to it—conceptualizing politics in a nonpartisan and candidate-centered fashion may well become a behavior pattern that could be difficult to alter.

The major objective of this book is to assess the extent of the decline of political partisanship in the electorate, the nature of the decline, and the reasons for it. The term "political partisanship" is a rather vague one, yet it is precisely because of this quality that I have chosen to use it, as it can be employed to refer to a broad range of public attitudes toward the parties. For too long research on the condition of parties in the electorate has concentrated almost solely on party identification. The research design employed here will emphasize using multiple methods to measure multiple traits of the public's attitudes toward the parties.

One limitation of the party identification scale is that one can only assess which party the respondent generally prefers and how strongly—it does not necessarily imply how positive, neutral, or negative people feel about the two parties. In order to understand what the distribution of party identification is likely to mean for the system, however, it is essential to know the evaluation nature of the attitudes on which it is based, that is, how each of the major alternatives are perceived. If we can ascertain what partisan preferences in the electorate represent about people's attitudes toward the parties, we will be much more likely to judge accurately what, if any, the long-term implications will be.

In addition to understanding the nature of the changes in the public's attitudes toward political parties, it is also important to know what has and what has not been an underlying cause of the changes which have occurred. If we want to know what, if anything, it will take to reverse the decline of partisanship in the electorate, we must first know what the sources of it have been. However, the causes of the decline are far less clear than the fact of the decline itself. Numerous possibilities have been discussed in the literature, but many are purely speculative and others leave key questions unanswered. A further shortcoming is that seldom has more than one explanation been considered and tested in the same analysis. Although not every conceivable factor can be examined here, a variety of possible factors will be explored, both for their theoretical significance and for their empirical plausibility.

This work is offered in the hope that it will add to our understanding of the American public's views of, and support for, the political parties. Because the study of party identification has contributed so heavily to what we know to date, it will be the major focus for the first few chapters. Next, other measures will be examined in order to provide a more in-depth understanding of the current state of political partisanship in the electorate and the nature of the changes that have taken place. Finally, the variables that may be responsible for the decline of partisanship will be examined.

1
The Concept of
Political Partisanship

"Despite there being a quite voluminous literature on partisanship as of the 1980s," Jack Dennis laments in a recent paper, "one looks in vain for any comprehensive statement of the theoretical meaning or purposes of the construct."[1] Perhaps the major reason for this shortcoming is that over the years many different scholars have used some variant of the concept for a wide variety of purposes. Furthermore, most of the working definitions of partisanship that have been employed have contained a high degree of construct validity. Thus, depending on the particular interests of the researcher, partisanship can take on numerous different theoretical meanings and purposes, thereby making it difficult for any single piece of research to treat the concept comprehensively. By devoting an entire book to the subject, it may be possible to at least partially overcome this difficulty.

Starting with the most practical purpose, partisanship can be used to predict voting behavior with a high degree of accuracy. Democrats tend to vote for Democratic candidates and Republicans tend to vote for Republican candidates. Such a pattern seemed so obvious to the

Columbia research group which conducted pioneering studies of voting in the 1940 and 1948 elections that they virtually ignored it.[2] Indeed, on the surface, to say that partisans usually vote for candidates from their own party seems tautological. If partisanship is no more than a reflection of voting intentions, why not address the question directly and just ask people how they will vote? Such a criticism has been the major focus of attention for many European scholars, who argue that because reports of party loyalty closely follow those of the vote, the concept of partisanship is not of much use in their countries.[3]

In the United States, however, one *can* clearly distinguish partisanship from voting behavior, as the correlation is far from perfect. What makes partisanship particularly interesting in the U.S. context, then, is not merely that it enables us to predict the vote, but also that it allows us to identify the situations in which voting behavior deviates from what we might normally expect. The fact that Jimmy Carter could have been expected to receive 55 percent of the two-party vote for president in 1980 based on the distribution of party identification in the electorate clearly does not reflect the election outcome very well, but it does give us a baseline from which to judge the magnitude of the candidate and issue factors that led to the Reagan victory.

In short, partisanship provides us with a means for distinguishing long-term from short-term change. Theoretically, its measurement taps a generalized standing decision on the part of the citizen to vote for a particular party under normal circumstances. Such a decision will of course not always be followed because circumstances are never completely "normal"; each election differs in many ways from the next in terms of the issues of the day and the candidates presented to the voters. However, because such factors influencing the vote usually last for only a short period of time, partisans are likely to return to the fold once such forces disappear from the political scene. A pattern in which individuals continue to be Democrats even though they voted for a particular Republican candidate (or vice versa) indicates that the shift in the vote is likely to be of short duration. In contrast, if the distribution of party loyalties also shifts, then what may seem to be a short-term change in the vote may in fact be an indication of a long-term change as well.

Such a theoretical framework for understanding voting behavior assumes that the distribution of partisanship in the electorate is more stable over time than election returns from year to year. This has undoubtedly been the case over the last three decades. Examining the presidential election returns from 1952 to 1980 leaves one with a distinct sense of the volatility of American electoral behavior. Except for the elections of 1952 and 1956, no two successive elections have produced anything approaching similar results. Close elections have alternated with landslides, and Democratic victories with Republican victories. In contrast, survey data from the Survey Research Center/Center for Political Studies (SRC/CPS) National Election Studies indicate a remarkable stability in the relative strength of the two parties nationwide in terms of psychological identification. Democrats have consistently outnumbered Republicans from 1952 to 1980 by an average ratio of approximately 1.7 to 1, which translates into an expected normal vote of roughly 54 percent Democratic when historical differences in turnout and defection rates are taken into account.[4] There has of course been some variation in this ratio over the years, but the standard deviation is only 1.7, compared to 7.0 for the actual vote. The stability of partisanship vis-à-vis the vote is also confirmed on the basis of individual-level panel data. For example, of the respondents in the 1972–1976 panel who voted in both presidential elections, 26 percent shifted their vote while only 7 percent changed their party affiliation from one party to the other.[5]

In sum, partisanship has been postulated in the political science literature as functioning as a preserving or stabilizing influence on public opinion, and consequently on the political system as well. According to Philip Converse and Georges Dupeux, the likelihood of voters' being attracted to "flash" parties and demagogic leaders is considerably lessened by the degree to which the citizens of a polity identify with one of the established parties.[6] It is naturally some sort of economic or cultural shock that leads to such sudden shifts of popular support, they write, but systems in which many voters do not have long-term partisan attachments are the most likely to be significantly affected.

The crucial assumption here is that partisanship represents a positive sense of affect toward one of the parties. This affect is often learned early in life from one's parents and theoretically grows stronger with age. What is most important is the psychological attachment involved, not any legal membership or contact with the party organization. Nevertheless, despite the stress on individual psychological dispositions, the group basis of partisanship was clearly central in the formulation of the well-known Michigan theory of party identification. As the authors of *The Voter Decides* wrote:

The present analysis of party identification is based on the assumption that the two parties serve as standard-setting groups for a significant proportion of the people of this country. In other words, it is assumed that many people associate themselves psychologically with one or the other of the parties, and that this identification has predictable relationships with their perceptions, evaluations and actions. These relationships would be expected to be in the areas of experience relevant to the activities of political parties.[7]

The emphasis on group attachment was further expanded upon by the Michigan scholars in *The American Voter:*

In characterizing the relation of individual to party as a psychological identification we invoke a concept that has played an important if somewhat varied role in psychological theories of the relation of individual to individual or of individual to group. We use the concept here to characterize the individual's affective orientation to an important group-object in his environment. Both reference group theory and small-group studies of influence have converged upon the attracting or repelling quality of the group as the generalized dimension most critical in defining the individual-group relationship, and it is this dimension that we call identification.[8]

Years later, Warren Miller noted that the term "identification" was "used quite intentionally to express the assumption that the relationship often involves an extension of ego." Generically, party identification is similar to religious identification: "In both instances the institution, that is the group, is concerned with defining the proper relationship between the person and the group-relevant components of social life. Indeed, the existence of the group, with acknowledged leaders who articulate the group's values and interpret the group's interest in the stream of public affairs, is crucial to the group member's ability to relate to the larger world."[9]

Party identification theoretically serves, then, as the primary source of *orientation* for an individual's political attitudes, just as religious denomination acts as an orientation for religious matters. Once one becomes psychologically attached to a party one tends to see political matters as other party members do. Being a Democrat therefore makes one more likely to give Democratic leaders the benefit of the doubt and to perceive issues in a Democratic light. Presumably, in many cases this is simply because of the identification itself rather than the result of a searching analysis of the candidates and current policy questions. (One of the key findings of the early Michigan voting studies was in fact the lack of political knowledge and involvement in the electorate.) In *The American Voter* such an effect of party identification was labeled a "perceptual screen"—through it one sees what is favorable to one's partisan orientation and filters out dissonant information. The stronger the party bond, the more likely the selection and distortion processes were found to be.

Partisanship thus plays a useful role for party leaders: it gives them a base of support in the electorate which can generally (within limits) be depended upon to view their actions in a favorable light. Just as the home team's fans will always tend to see the referee's close calls in favor of the home team, so will partisans support their party leaders in questionable cases.

The perceptual screening involved in party identification also facilitates the task of holding together the unusually diverse party coalitions that the American two-party system necessarily generates. Research has demon-strated that party identifiers adjust, or project, their per-ceptions of where the parties stand on issues in such a way that their own issue beliefs match those of their cho-sen party.[10] In other words, conservative Democrats will be more likely to see the Democratic Party as leaning to-ward conservative stands while liberal Democrats will be more likely to see the party as leaning in a liberal di-rection. The net result is to reduce the psychological issue distance between individuals and their respective parties, thereby giving party leaders room to maneuver within a limited issue space rather than tying them to fixed and uncompromisable positions.

In spite of these theoretical benefits to the political sys-tem, the process of perceptual screening involved in par-tisanship has often been interpreted by scholars as an indication that democracy in the United States is not functioning properly. If issue positions are merely the re-sult of party identification, then what we may have is more of a *rationalizing* voter than a rational one, accord-ing to this line of thought. On the other hand, however, there clearly is a rationalistic aspect to party identifica-tion, which along with the group basis of the concept has received a good deal of attention in the literature. Elec-toral politics is inordinately more complicated and time-consuming for the average citizen in the United States than for those in almost any other democratic country in the world. First of all, Americans are expected to vote for a plethora of political offices including president, senator, representative, governor, state senator, state representa-tive, mayor, city council members, school board members, sheriff, drain commissioner, and a host of others, depend-ing on the locality. Second, American voters are asked to exercise their franchise unusually often. While the typical European voter may be called upon to cast two or three ballots in a four-year period, many Americans are faced with a dozen or more separate elections in the space of four years.[11]

To make a rough analogy, it would probably take an individual approximately the amount of time required for one or two college-level courses a year in order to cast a completely informed vote for all of these offices in all of these elections. Therefore, voters need shortcuts, or cues, such as partisanship to facilitate their decision-making. As Anthony Downs writes, "It may be rational for a man to delegate part or all of his political decision-making to others, no matter how important it is that he make correct decisions."[12] Given that the two parties do consistently offer fairly distinctive (if not diametrically opposing) alternatives, delegating one's vote along party lines tends to facilitate representation even though one may know absolutely nothing about the particular issue stands of the candidates who are on the ballot.[13]

Those who stress the rational basis of party identification usually concentrate on the cognitive side of partisanship rather than on the affective link emphasized in *The American Voter*. Such analysts construe party loyalties as largely a reflection of people's evaluations of the past and current performance of the two parties. For example, Fiorina defines party identification as "the difference between an individual's past political experiences with the two parties ... Past political experiences, of course, are simply the voters subjectively weighted retrospective evaluations formed while observing the postures and performances of the contending parties during previous election periods."[14] Within such a framework, partisanship is both an exogenous and an endogenous variable. In other words, not only will one's identification affect how one views political issues and leaders, but so also will the short-term forces affect party identification. Making use of the available panel data on party identification, some scholars have concluded that variation over time on the individual level, far from being random noise, follows predictable patterns on the basis of recent party fortunes, new issues, or changes in existing issue preferences.[15] As Charles Franklin and John Jackson write, "In this way, each campaign leaves its imprint, or residue, on individual identifications."[16] Thus, from a cognitive psychological perspective, partisanship can be postulated as serving as an economizing or storage device, enabling the individual to keep a running scorecard on the performance of the two parties in order to guide his or her voting decisions.

Finally, partisanship has also been viewed as encompassing a variety of normative attitudes regarding the role that political parties should play in the American governmental system. The formal theory for this view has best been expressed by Herbert Weisberg, who argues that party identification should be viewed as a multidimensional concept that taps separate attitudes toward the Democratic and Republican parties, political independence, and political parties in general.[17] In short, partisanship may stand for support for the *institution* of the political party as well as support for a particular party.

Data from the 1980 national election study make it possible to test such an assumption on a nationwide scale thoroughly for the first time. As Table 1.1 shows, party identifiers were far more likely than nonpartisans to express support for a variety of aspects concerning political parties as institutions. Weak partisanship and espe-

Table 1.1 Normative attitudes toward political parties

	Strong partisans	Weak partisans	Non-partisans[a]
The truth is, we probably don't need political parties in America anymore.			
Agree	20.9	30.2	42.6
Pro-con	6.3	13.0	13.3
Disagree	72.8	56.8	44.1
It would be better if in all elections we put no party labels on the ballot.			
Agree	33.9	44.8	59.8
Pro-con	9.0	14.7	36.5
Disagree	57.1	36.5	27.6
The parties do more to confuse the issues than to provide a clear choice on the issues.			
Agree	46.0	56.6	62.2
Pro-con	16.1	24.2	20.1
Disagree	37.9	19.2	17.7
It is better to be a firm party supporter than to be a political independent.			
Agree	61.6	32.5	10.9
Pro-con	15.5	15.9	9.8
Disagree	22.9	51.6	79.2
The best rule in voting is to pick a candidate regardless of party label.			
Agree	58.6	74.2	82.9
Pro-con	9.2	9.9	5.6
Disagree	32.3	15.9	11.4

a. Independent leaners are combined here with pure Independents, as no significant differences were found on any of these questions.
SOURCE: 1980 CPS National Election Study.

cially independence are associated with feelings that parties are unnecessary in our system, that they do more to confuse than to clarify issues, and that one should vote for the man and not the party. It is interesting to note, however, that such attitudes are quite widespread even among strong partisans. For example, more of these respondents agreed than disagreed with the statements that parties confuse the issues and that the best rule in voting is to pick a candidate regardless of party label. Patterns such as these have prompted Jack Dennis to write that "we may be called upon in the not so distant future to witness the demise of a once prominent institution of American government and politics,"[18] that is, the political party.

Americans have always tended to view parties rather ambivalently, however, beginning with the Founding Fathers.[19] Thus in order to make even a preliminary assessment of assertions of the demise of partisanship in the electorate, the empirical evidence over time must be carefully examined. Two well-known classes of evidence will be looked at—one concerning the changing relationship of party to the vote and the other dealing with the frequency and strength of party identification over time.

The Decline of Party Voting

Although sample survey evidence is necessarily limited to the relatively recent period for which data are available, one can take a far more extended historical perspective on partisanship and its relation to the vote by examining aggregate election returns over time. We would expect that if party loyalties are closely related to the vote, the results for different offices in the same election should closely parallel one another. Therefore, if a Democratic candidate wins the race in a given district for president, then other Democratic candidates in the district should also win. If, however, voters are casting their ballots on the basis of factors other than party, ticket-splitting may result in victories for some candidates on the ticket and losses for others. Such a phenomenon has been termed "electoral disaggregation" by Walter Dean Burnham, whose *Critical Elections and the Mainsprings of American Politics* offers one of the most comprehensive treatments of aggregate historical voting patterns.[20]

Perhaps the most often quoted statistic that Burnham uses to demonstrate the growth of electoral disaggregation is the percentage of districts in which there is a split in the outcome for the presidential versus the congressional race. Because the unit of analysis is identical from election to election and every part of the country can be incorporated in the analysis, such a measure seems to be reasonably consistent over time and capable of tapping national trends. As Figure 1.1 shows, the proportion of split results has risen quite markedly over the last sixty years. Only about 10 to 15 percent of the 435 congressional districts had split results in the 1920–1944 period. In the twenty years between 1944 and 1964, however, this figure gradually rose to about 30 percent. And in 1972 one finds an all-time high of 44 percent, which indicates that the occurrence of an identical outcome for both races was hardly any greater than would be expected by chance.

Of course these data are subject to aggregate fallacy: one could theoretically find many people splitting their tickets in a district where the outcome in both races is nevertheless similar, or alternatively one could find a split result caused by only a few people crossing party lines.[21] However, the data do provide an indication that the decline in straight-ticket voting may have begun before the first SRC national election study in 1952. Furthermore, such a pattern almost certainly rules out the possibility that any increase in split-ticket voting found subsequent

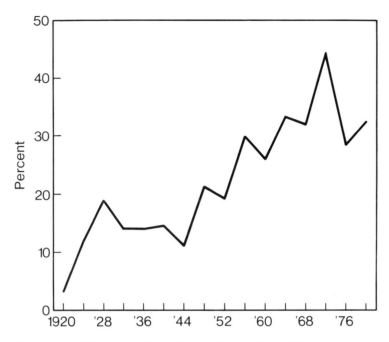

Figure 1.1   Districts with split presidential and House results, 1920–1980

Sources: Data for 1920–1976 taken from John F. Bibby, Thomas E. Mann, and Norman J. Ornstein, *Vital Statistics on Congress, 1980* (Washington, D.C.: American Enterprise Institute, 1980); 1980 data calculated by the author from election returns.

to the early election studies is merely a return to normalcy.

Examining the individual-level survey data from the period between 1952 and 1980 confirms the conclusion from the aggregate statistics that the degree of electoral disaggregation has risen quite sharply over the last few decades. As Warren Miller and Teresa Levitan have rightly argued, one possible reason for the increase in ticket-splitting is simply that specific presidential candidates have been nominated whom many party members could not support.[22] However, the fact that secular increases are found even in measures that do not involve presidential voting strongly indicates the presence of a true behavioral trend. Comparing the two end points in the time series one finds that:

1. The proportion of voters reporting that they have voted for different parties in presidential elections has risen from 29 to 57 percent.
2. Ticket-splitting between presidential and House candidates has increased from 12 to 34 percent.
3. Ticket-splitting between House and Senate candidates has grown from 9 to 31 percent.
4. The proportion of voters splitting their tickets in elections for other state and local offices has gone from 27 to 59 percent.

The survey data trends displayed in Figure 1.2, however, do not exactly parallel the aggregate data shown in Figure 1.1. Despite the change between 1952 and 1960 in the proportion of split results on the district level, the individual-level data indicate very little change during this period. Conversely, after 1964 the aggregate data appear fairly stable, except for the short-lived increase in 1972; the individual-level data, on the other hand, show a continued steady increase on all four measures through 1980.

The contrasts between the survey evidence and the aggregate voting patterns suggest caution in interpreting even major across-the-board gains for one party as necessarily indicating a resurgence of partisanship. For example, the fact that Ronald Reagan's victory in 1980, unlike that of Richard Nixon's in 1972, was accompanied by large gains for the Republicans in both the House and the

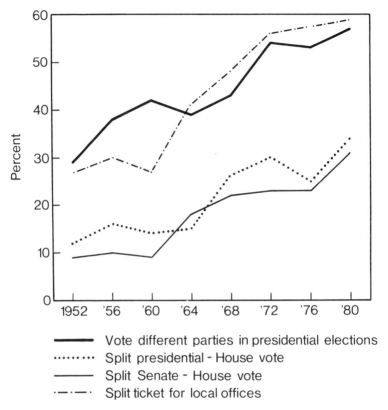

Figure 1.2   Trends in split-ticket voting, 1952–1980
Source: SRC/CPS National Election Studies.

Senate has led many to speculate that the era of ticket-splitting may be coming to an end. Even the noted Democratic pollster Patrick Caddell, whose political position might predispose him toward alternative explanations for his party's congressional losses in 1980, has noted the apparent return of coattail voting. "A continuation of this trend," writes Caddell, "could be a positive development for both parties, and an opportunity for one or the other—or even both—to strengthen its weak grip on the public."[23] Yet it is clear from the data shown in Figure 1.2 that the apparent rise in straight-ticket voting in 1980 was merely an optical illusion, and that on the behavioral level the parties' grip on the electorate in fact reached a new all-time low.

Furthermore, given the current state of public attitudes concerning party-line voting, there is good reason to expect that the process of electoral disaggregation may continue for some time to come. The attitudinal potential for ticket-splitting has consistently been greater than its incidence, and as such one can reasonably interpret recent trends as reflecting the tendency for behaviors eventually to come into line with attitudes. In 1952, for instance, the SRC election study posed the following question to respondents: "Some people think that if a voter votes for one party for President he should vote for the same party for Senator and Congressman. Do you agree or disagree with this statement?" Although over 80 percent of the voters reported casting such a party-line vote, only 40 percent agreed with the statement. Similarly, Jack Dennis reports that a 1956 Gallup poll found that 74 percent of the public thought one should vote for the person rather than the party; in 1968 the figure was 84 percent.[24] And finally, in the 1980 election study respondents were asked to agree or disagree on a seven-point scale with the statement, "The best rule in voting is to pick a candidate regardless of party label." The results reveal not only that such a view is widely held, but also that it is held with great intensity by many:

Disagree						*Agree*
1	2	3	4	5	6	7
9%	4%	5%	8%	11%	21%	41%

To recapitulate, it is clear that partisanship has declined substantially from the perspective of its ability to structure the vote. Ticket-splitting has assumed massive proportions compared to the rate just two decades ago, and only a small minority of the electorate now believes that one should vote strictly on the basis of party labels.

The Decline of Party Identification

Accompanying the trend toward greater split-ticket voting there has also been a decline in party identification. Election studies during the period from 1952 to 1964 consistently found that approximately 75 percent of the electorate identified themselves as either Democrats or Republicans, and roughly half of these identifiers considered themselves to be strong partisans. The similarity in the party identification marginals from one sample survey to another during this period led Philip Converse to write of the "serene stability in the distribution of party loyalties" expressed by the public,[25] and later to call these years the "steady state period" with regard to party identification.[26] Figure 1.3 shows that after 1964 the picture changed somewhat, however. Between 1964 and 1972 the percentage of respondents identifying with one of the two major parties declined from 77 to 64 percent. In addition, people who continued to identify with a party after 1964 expressed a weaker sense of identification than previously. Although strong partisans were almost as numerous as weak partisans from 1952 to 1964, by 1972 the latter outnumbered the former by a ratio of slightly over three to two.

At first, these changes in the distribution of party loyalties were seen as quite a revolutionary development. For example, Burnham wrote that the losses in identification

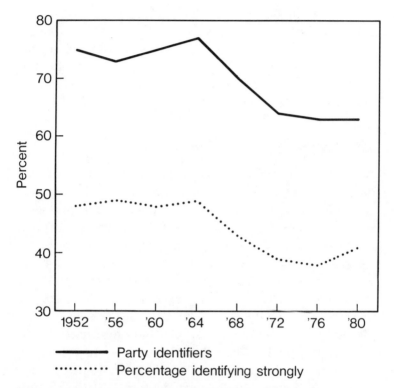

Party identifiers
Percentage identifying strongly

Figure 1.3 Decline in party identification, 1952–1980
Source: SRC/CPS National Election Studies.

for both parties could very well represent "a dissolution
of the parties as action intermediaries in electoral choice
and other politically relevant acts." In addition, the rise of
a "mass base for independent political movements of
ideological tone and considerable long-term staying
power" seemed to be one possible consequence of the decline, according to Burnham.[27] Similarly, Gerald Pomper
wrote that the continuation of such a trend "may eventually bring the nation to a free-floating politics, in which

prediction is hazardous, continuities are absent, and governmental responsibility is impossible to fix."[28] In Pomper's view, the implications for democracy seemed quite threatening.

More recently, however, a revisionist view has come into prominence; it perceives the decline in party identification as far less cataclysmic. To begin with, the downward trend no longer seems to be a trend at all, but rather a limited period effect in which there was a rapid decline followed by the development of a new level of stability. Furthermore, the period of weakening party loyalties— 1964 to 1972—was clearly an unusually tumultuous epoch in the history of American politics, which may well never again be duplicated in the severity of the shocks (Vietnam, racial unrest, and so on) felt by the electorate.[29]

Perhaps more important is the analytic argument by Bruce Keith et al. that the decline in party identification has been vastly exaggerated by considering as nonpartisans Independents who report that they think of themselves as closer to one of the two parties.[30] These so-called "Independent leaners" are not an uncommitted and unmobilized bloc, according to these scholars, but are instead largely "closet" Democrats and Republicans. Although they may prefer to call themselves Independents than Democrats or Republicans, when it comes to their voting behavior in presidential elections they tend to act just as partisan as weak party identifiers. Between 1952 and 1980 the mean defection rate for weak Democrats was 35 percent, compared to 34 percent for Independent Democrats; likewise, weak Republicans defected 16 percent of the time on the average, compared to 15 percent for Independent Republicans.[31] If one therefore considers Independent leaners as simply partisans by another name, then the proportion of the population identifying with a party can hardly be said to have declined at all over the years. As Keith et al. write, "Most of the growth in Independents has occurred among the hidden partisans, while the high-level speculations have concerned the genuine Independents, whose increase has been rather modest."[32]

From a somewhat different perspective, Philip Converse and Gregory Markus have also made a major contribution to the school of thought which argues that the erosion of partisan ties has not been as sharp as people such as Burnham or Pomper would have us believe.[33] One of the most important early findings concerning the concept of party identification was that the stability in individual placement on the scale far exceeded the stability of any other attitudinal variable in the 1956–1960 election study panel. Such a pattern led Converse to conclude that party identification was clearly the most central attitude in the mass public's political belief system.[34]

Subsequent writings that argued the case for the destabilization of party identification, however, did so without the benefit of more recent panel data in order to test whether party loyalties had in fact become more volatile. The conclusion seemed logical, given the changes that had occurred since the 1950s, but yet it remained purely speculative. It was not until the completion of a second long-term panel study, undertaken between 1972 and 1976, that a direct test of the proposition became possible. And as Converse and Markus reported, the massive change that might have been expected was not at all confirmed. The average two-year continuity correlation for party identification was found to be .813 in this later period compared to .835 during the 1956–1960 period. Therefore, despite the fact that strength of party identification has declined somewhat, Converse and Markus conclude that it continues to be the most stable object of political orientation, followed by evaluations of major presidential candidates and issue positions.[35]

Taking into account all of the recent revisionist points concerning the decline of party identification, it appears that the rise of split-ticket voting has been a much sharper and long-lasting trend. Therefore, it follows logically that a good portion of the increase in electoral disaggregation has been due to partisans' using their identifications less and less as a cue in voting behavior.[36] One possible explanation for such a pattern is that perhaps party identification simply means less to people across all levels than in the past. That is, continued identification with a party may not necessarily imply a continued high degree of importance for the identification.

The major problem with such an interpretation, of course, is Converse and Markus's argument that party identification remains the most *stable* political attitude among the mass public, with hardly any visible sign of a decline at all in this respect. But does stability necessarily indicate centrality? Certainly the reverse is true—that is, instability points to a lack of centrality—but there is no reason to believe that stability is by itself *prima facie* evidence for centrality. The fact that party identification has declined in its importance as a shaper of thought and determiner of opinion implies that the centrality of the labels of Democrat, Independent, and Republican may be far less than one might be led to believe by their across-time stability. In the next chapter we shall examine the stability question in greater detail by broadening the analysis to other pieces of data about public attitudes toward the parties, all of which call into question whether partisan attitudes are in fact uniquely central to the electorate.

2
The Stability of Partisan Attitudes

Despite the great reliability associated with the measurement of party identification, there has of late been a flurry of research activity criticizing the construct validity of the traditional seven-point scale. Specifically, it has been argued that the unidimensionality implicit in the construction of the scale is inappropriate because it assumes that partisanship and independence are mutually exclusive alternatives and that an individual must be one or the other.[1] These scholars maintain that party identification should be viewed as a multidimensional concept that involves components of partisan direction and strength *as well as a nonpartisanship component.*

For our purposes, the multidimensionality of party identification is particularly relevant because it raises questions about which dimension, or dimensions, of the scale account for its reliability. Is the high continuity correlation for the party identification measure due mostly to the stability of evaluative attitudes about the two parties or to attitudes of nonpartisanship? Only the former can be used as even inferential evidence for the centrality of party over other political attitudes.

From the early writings on independence, the concept of nonpartisanship was established in the discipline as a rather unstable attitude. For example, in an article devoted to the measurement and characteristics of independence, Samuel Eldersveld described Independents as "the segment of the electorate which is highly irregular in party allegiance."[2] Contrary to the normative ideal of the Independent as one who carefully weighs the appeals of both parties on the basis of all the available information, they were invariably found to be less informed about, and involved in, politics than party identifiers. As Campbell et al. stated, "The individual who has a strong and continuing involvement in politics is likely to develop a commitment to one or the other of the major parties."[3]

Under this framework, nonpartisanship was considered as quite often just a temporary phase one might go through before settling with one of the parties as one's "standing decision." However, it is one of the key points of this book that as political parties have become less salient to the electorate, a lack of party identification has increasingly come to represent a sense of *indifference* toward both the Democrats and the Republicans. Thus, given that Independents are relatively unconcerned with political parties, their nonpartisanship may be just as stable as the partisanship of Democratic and Republican identifiers. Such a hypothesis is in fact nicely confirmed by data from the 1980 election study panel, in which all respondents were asked separately whether they considered themselves a supporter of one of the political parties and whether they ever thought of themselves as a political independent. Between January and September 78 percent responded identically to the party support question compared to 75 percent on the question of political independence.

Thus the party identification scale is probably not entirely appropriate to measure whether evaluations of political parties are the most central of all political orientations. The stability of nonpartisanship indicates the lack of centrality of parties for the respondent, yet it contributes to a correlation that has been widely interpreted as demonstrating the continued importance of partisan attitudes. Therefore, we shall turn to more direct measures of evaluations of each of the two parties in order to test whether such an interpretation is in fact warranted.

Feeling Thermometer Ratings of the Parties

One particularly useful methodological device for comparing the stability of evaluations of a variety of political objects is the feeling thermometer. Through the use of the standardized zero-to-one-hundred scale, comparability problems in question wording are greatly reduced. One does not have to worry whether the possible alternatives in the question are worded better than in another—only whether the stimuli ("Democrats," "Liberals," and so on) are phrased sensibly.

Converse and Markus have examined the stability of thermometer ratings of presidential candidates in the 1972–1976 panel and found that the continuity correlations for candidates fall significantly below the correlation for party identification. However, when one examines ratings of "Democrats" and "Republicans," the continuity correlations are actually somewhat *lower* than those for most leaders:

Ted Kennedy	.67	*Democrats*	.47
George Wallace	.62	Richard Nixon	.45
George McGovern	.54	*Republicans*	.43
Hubert Humphrey	.53	Henry Jackson	.34

Thus, by squaring the correlations, we find that ratings of Ted Kennedy between 1972 and 1976 shared 45 percent common variance compared to only 22 percent for ratings of "Democrats."

One possible problem with such a finding is that the wording of "Democrats" and "Republicans" is a bit ambiguous. Respondents might quite reasonably personalize the referent to include friends and neighbors as well as specific party leaders. Fortunately, one can assess the stability of ratings of the Democratic and Republican *parties* based on collection of panel data in January and September of 1980. These data show a slightly better picture for the stability of partisan attitudes, but again one finds that the continuity correlations are not any higher than for evaluations of political leaders:

Ted Kennedy	.69	Ronald Reagan	.54
Democratic Party	.65	*Republican Party*	.54
Gerald Ford	.63	Walter Mondale	.52
Jimmy Carter	.61	Jerry Brown	.49
George Wallace	.60	Howard Baker	.44
George McGovern	.59	George Bush	.39
John Connally	.58		

Clearly, the interpretation indicated by the feeling thermometer data is that although party identification is a uniquely stable attitudinal variable, evaluations of political parties are not. One reason why party identification is so stable over time is undoubtedly that unlike most other attitudinal variables it involves a process of self-labeling. However, the fact that party evaluations are no more stable than candidate evaluations implies that these labels are not as salient to individual respondents as one might infer from the high degree of reliability associated with them. It has often been argued that although the reliability of public responses to issue questions is extremely low, the underlying opinions are nevertheless quite stable.[4] In this case just the reverse seems true—the responses are far more stable than the underlying attitudes that they supposedly represent.

The question that this finding naturally raises is whether such has always been the case or whether the stability of evaluations of the parties has in fact declined over time. In order to investigate this question we need to compare the stability of evaluations of the parties in the 1956–1960 panel to that in the 1972–1976 panel.

Decline in the Stability of Party Evaluations over Time

Unfortunately, the 1956–1960 panel was conducted before the introduction of the feeling thermometer into the election studies, so it is impossible to determine whether the stability of these ratings has declined over the years. However, both the 1956–1960 panel and the 1972–1976 panel contain identical open-ended questions that ask respondents what they like and dislike about each of the two parties. By counting the number of likes and then subtracting the number of dislikes, one can create summary scores that represent respondents' evaluations of the two parties.[5]

As hypothesized, the results show that on these measures the continuity correlations have fallen over time. In the 1956–1960 panel the continuity correlation for evaluations of the Democratic Party was .51; by the 1972–1976 panel this figure had fallen to .41. Similarly, for evaluations of the Republican Party one finds a decline in stability from .50 in the early panel study to .39 in the more recent study. Finally, in order to more closely approximate the bipolar nature of the party identification scale it is possible to create a party-affect scale by constructing a difference measure between each respondent's evaluations of the two parties. This measure yields somewhat higher correlations within each panel but again shows a decline over time—from .61 in 1956–1960 to .50 in 1972–1976.

Although these changes may not seem to be much on the surface, if one examines the percentage of variance explained, the decline in the stability of party evaluations is between 30 and 40 percent in the space of a decade and a half. Such a trend, furthermore, is more than just a reflection of the decline in strength of party identification. It is true that in both panels the stronger one's party identification the more likely one is to evaluate the parties consistently over time. However, except in the case of pure Independents, each level of strength of party identification shows a substantial decline in stability of party evaluations from the 1950s to the 1970s.

Generational replacement and the lowering of the voting age also do not provide much of an explanation. Given the fact that older people evaluate the parties with more stability than younger respondents, one might, under normal circumstances, expect to find that as age cohorts pass through the life-cycle the consistency of their evaluations should increase. In the period between the two long-term panels, however, just the opposite trend is found to have occurred within each cohort. This is not to say that the decline in strength of party identification and the influx of young voters has not had an effect on the overall stability of party evaluations by the electorate. Both trends have indeed increased the proportion of people whom we would expect to have the least stable evaluations. However, the important point to note is that the greater instability in party evaluations is independent of each, and therefore indicative of a previously unrecognized change in the nature of public attitudes toward the political parties.

The results of this chapter lead us to question the esteemed position of partisan attitudes in the literature on voting behavior. Upon closer scrutiny it has been found that political parties are not the most stable objects of political orientation after all; both partisans and nonpartisans no longer evaluate the parties as consistently as they did in the past. Party identification may be just as stable overall as it was two decades ago, but nevertheless political parties no longer mean as much to people as they once did, as evidenced by the decline in the stability of party evaluations. What the growth in the popularity of the label "Independent" means has not been very well established, however. That will be the major task of the next chapter.

3
Independent or No Preference?

Political independence has probably been the most intensely scrutinized and debated aspect of the concept of party identification. Although the partisan balance has remained relatively stable for decades, the proportion of Americans known as "Independents" has risen substantially since the mid-1960s. Because citizens who do not identify with a political party are generally seen as holding the balance of power, such an increase is both strategically significant for those concerned with winning elections and theoretically significant for scholars concerned with the stability of the American party system. Much academic discussion has centered on the generational makeup of this group,[1] their political sophistication,[2] and the possibility that many may in fact be "closet partisans."[3]

Throughout all of this controversy and debate, however, one central and substantively relevant methodological point has been largely ignored—namely, that a respondent does not necessarily have to say that he or she is an Independent to be classified as such. Virtually all of the research that has been done using the standard measure of party identification has employed the derived scale without any analysis of the different paths by which it is possible to reach the same point on the scale. Yet, as Philip Converse has written, there is a small but significant fraction of the American population to whom "the notion of an abiding loyalty to a political party which underlies the party identification measure is next to meaningless. When posed the party identification question in an interview situation, many of this remnant give responses which properly get them coded as 'apolitical' or, as is a bit more misleading, as 'Independents.' "[4]

It is the central argument of this chapter that the "remnant" Converse describes is no longer just a remnant. In fact, the growth of this group in recent years accounts for most of the increase in the Independent categories on the party identification scale. Such a trend, however, is not an indication of an increase in the proportion of traditional apoliticals, who have virtually no interest in politics, but rather is yet another indication of the declining importance of political parties in the eyes of the American public.

Perhaps the most fundamental premise of the concept of independence is that there is something which one is independent *from*. In the case of political independence this is of course the political parties. It is one of the key hypotheses of this study, however, that political parties have been becoming increasingly meaningless to the electorate since the early 1950s. Thus the question of either identifying with one of the parties or being independent from both may be considerably less relevant to respondents than in the past and therefore much more likely to draw the simple answer "I don't have any preference at all." The difference between this response and saying

"I'm an Independent" may seem to be a subtle one, given that both represent a lack of partisanship, but the interpretation of party decline in the electorate is quite different when one takes into account the fact that the former type of response has been increasing far more rapidly than the latter. Instead of representing a conscious decision on the part of many to disdain from partisan labels, such a finding suggests that the decline of party identification has more likely resulted from a decrease in the salience of parties as attitudinal objects in the United States. What we are thus witnessing is the rise of a type of nonpartisan that the party identification scale cannot distinguish—one who is somewhat aware of political matters but lacks responsiveness to the concepts of either partisanship or independence.

The Increase in "No Preference"

The lead question in the party identification sequence is perhaps the best known in the history of survey research. If there were a Hall of Fame for mass survey questions, there is no doubt that "Generally speaking, do you usually consider yourself a Democrat, a Republican, an Independent, or what?" would be enshrined in it. Yet coding the responses to the question is not as simple as one might expect from its closed-ended nature, for not everyone chooses one of the three categories enumerated in the question. Many respond in such a way that they are initially coded as having no preference, given that they don't consider any of the labels in the question as applicable to them. A few examples from the interview protocols (some of which are quite common, others of which are obviously idiosyncratic) will help illustrate the type of responses frequently obtained from these individuals:

"Nothing in that respect. I don't consider myself anything politically."

"I ain't none of them."

"None."

"Not anything."

[Laughs.] "You should call me nothing."

"No preference."

"I don't think of myself as anything."

"It depends."

"I'm an American [citizen]."

"Oh hell, I don't know."

"May the best man win. It's the best candidate."

[Interviewer asks if respondent would call himself an Independent.] "You don't mean one of those minority groups?"

"I'm a person who believes in what I believe is a good man who will do the most for the country."

[Interviewer repeats question.] "I'm not a Republican, not a Democrat, not an Independent, and not a Communist."

"I'm nothing. I don't holler about it."

These comments suggest that the party identification question lacked substantive meaning for these people and that none of the choices offered was seen by them as a relevant political reference point. Yet each of these respondents was eventually coded as an Independent on the party identification scale.

How do such people end up as Independents even though they fail to identify themselves as such? In the case of those who are categorized as pure Independents, the decision is based on the respondent's interest in politics. Respondents are classified as apoliticals *only* if they (1) express no preference to the initial party identification question; (2) say that they do not lean toward either party; and (3) show little interest in politics. If after meeting the first two criteria the respondent shows interest in politics, he or she is moved *by the election study staff* to the pure Independent slot on the scale; the apolitical classification is reserved only for those who are almost totally uninterested and uninformed about politics.

Through 1964 such judgments by the election study staff were made largely on the basis of how the respondents reacted to the question, as there was a full line on the interview schedule to record each individual's answer. After 1964 the format of the interview protocol was changed slightly by printing boxes for the interviewer to check ("Democrat," "Republican," "Independent," "no preference," "other party"). Beginning in 1966, therefore, the interviewers could simply check the "no preference" box without recording the actual response, which made it necessary for the study staff to skim through the rest of the protocol to determine whether the person was interested in politics or not.[5]

In the case of those who indicate a lack of any preference on the initial question but who state that they lean toward one of the two parties, the coding has always been a clear-cut procedure. These people are automatically classified as Independent leaners despite the fact that *they have not identified themselves* as Independents. Yet many in this group really do not consider themselves as anything politically and merely pick a partisan leaning under the pressure of the interview situation. In one example of this phenomenon, a respondent in the 1964 study answered "I don't know" to the lead party identification question and then, in response to the question of whether she leaned toward either party, asked the interviewer

which party Johnson represented and which Goldwater
was from. When the interviewer explained the situation
(contrary to accepted interviewing procedures), the respondent then said that she leaned toward the Democrats.
Such a response, rather than revealing a long-term psychological disposition, clearly has more to do with the respondent's short-term intentions.

In all, there are five categories of nonpartisans to be examined. First, there are the traditional apoliticals for
whom the party identification question has little meaning
and who simply are not at all interested in politics. Then
there are the two groups who are not classified as apoliticals but who express no preference to the lead question—
one of these groups leans toward neither party and the
other group does indicate a partisan leaning. Finally, there
are the two groups of people who actually identify themselves as Independents—nonleaners and leaners.[6]

Table 3.1 shows the proportion of the population in
each of these five categories in presidential election years
from 1964 to 1980, the period heralded as that of the rise of
independence.[7] The data show that the increase in self-
classified Independents was quite real between 1964 and
1968. In both years the two no-preference categories were
quite negligible, representing less than 10 percent of all
those classified as Independents on the party identification scale. However, between 1968 and 1976 the proportion of self-classified or "real" Independents increased
very little, and the 1980 figures show a clear decline to
below the comparable 1968 levels. In contrast, the two
no-preference categories have increased steadily since
1968 to the point where they now combine to represent
nearly 10 percent of the population and 30 percent of the
Independents on the scale as traditionally derived.[8] When

Table 3.1 Trends in the proportions of nonpartisan groups

Year	Apoliticals	No-preference neither	No-preference leaner	Independent neither	Independent leaner
1964	0.9	1.1	1.0	6.7	13.9
1968	1.4	1.2	1.3	9.3	17.2
1972	1.4	3.7	2.6	9.4	18.6
1976	0.9	4.4	2.6	10.0	18.6
1980	2.2	5.2	4.5	7.7	16.7

SOURCE: SRC/CPS National Election Studies.

these respondents are removed from the Independent category, we find the self-labeled Independents are hardly
any more numerous now than during the era that Converse has labeled as the steady-state period of strength of
partisanship.

Are They Apoliticals?

The major question that this finding raises is whether citizens in the two no-preference categories should in fact be
considered apoliticals rather than Independents. Table 3.2
shows that on a variety of measures of political involvement, based on pooled data from the 1964, 1968, 1972,
1976, and 1980 studies,[9] they are not strictly one or the
other. Compared to the respondents who have always
been classified as apoliticals, they vote more frequently,
have greater interest in the campaign, and have a higher
level of subjective political competence or internal effi-
cacy. Thus they are hardly so far removed from politics as
to be rightly considered apolitical. On the other hand,
they are not nearly as involved in politics as the self-
identified Independents. In sum, one finds the following
roughly linear progression of political involvement: (1)
apoliticals; (2) no-preference neithers; (3) no-preference
leaners; (4) pure Independents; and (5) Independent
leaners. Therefore, the two no-preference groups should
be considered separately as containing people who are
detached from the party system but yet not uninterested
enough in the political process as a whole to be classified
as complete apoliticals. Because they differ from those
who have traditionally been coded as apoliticals, as well
as those who identify themselves as Independents, we
will refer to them as "no-preference nonpartisans," so as

Table 3.2 Political involvement of nonpartisan groups, pooled 1964–1980 data (column percents)

	Apoliticals	No-preference neither	No-preference leaner	Independent neither	Independent leaner
Reported turnout					
Didn't vote	83.6	59.8	44.0	36.2	30.8
Voted	16.4	40.2	56.0	63.8	69.2
Frequency of voting					
Never	69.5	31.8	27.4	21.9	12.9
Sometimes	23.4	26.5	21.0	18.6	14.7
Most of the time	1.7	15.7	18.9	19.0	20.6
All of the time	5.4	26.0	32.6	40.6	51.8
Interest in the campaign					
Not much	80.8	43.4	29.5	31.5	19.9
Somewhat	17.3	41.9	44.3	43.2	45.6
Very much	1.9	14.7	26.3	25.3	34.6
Internal political efficacy					
Low (0–1)	79.6	70.4	66.6	63.1	50.8
High (2–3)	20.4	29.6	33.4	36.9	49.2

SOURCE: SRC/CPS National Election Studies.

to differentiate them from the categories obtained with the standard SRC/CPS coding scheme.

A Problem of Question Wording?

Perhaps, though, "no preference" is just what people say when they are confused by the choices in the standard party identification question. Following this line of reasoning, we might hypothesize that if no-preference nonpartisans were simply asked whether they ever considered themselves political Independents, they would acknowledge such an identity. Just such a question was in fact asked during the 1980 study in a section of the questionnaire separate from the usual party identification question. The results reveal some support for the above hypothesis, but the differences between the no-preference groups and the self-classified Independents are nevertheless quite marked. For example, only 24.5 percent of those who had "no preference" and leaned toward neither party responded that they sometimes considered themselves political Independents, compared to 75.4 percent of the respondents who called themselves "Independents" and leaned toward neither party. Similarly, only 38.4 percent of the no-preference leaners considered themselves to be political independents, compared to 82.7 percent of the Independent leaners.[10]

It is apparent, then, that the existence of this sizable block of no-preference nonpartisans is not simply an artifact of confused question wording. These respondents are distinct in their level of political involvement, and their attitudes toward political independence are different from those of self-professed Independents. Of course, it may be that these people could be readily categorized as a distinct group if the party identification question included a "no preference" option. Therefore, in this sense one can point to problems of question wording, in that the traditional version of the party identification scale does not provide an appropriate classification for these respondents.

Dissatisfaction with Parties or Indifference?

In order to develop a more complete understanding of party decline in the electorate, it is crucial to recognize that the proportion of people without a preference for the labels of Democrat, Republican, or Independent is both sizable and has been on the increase. Given that the growth in the proportion of no-preference nonpartisans has been so much more rapid than the growth of self-identified Independents, it is important to examine how differently the two groups perceive political parties. One possibility is that those with "no preference" are the most vehemently opposed to the political parties and dissatisfied with their performance. An alternative explanation is that these respondents do not perceive parties as relevant to the political process, and hence many of them do not consider themselves to be Independents simply because in their minds there are no meaningful partisan objects to be independent from.

Table 3.3 addresses both of these possibilities on the basis of three items that were asked about political parties in the 1980 CPS election study. One can test the first hypothesis by examining how the no-preference and Independent groups evaluate the job that the political parties are doing. Contrary to the hypothesis, the former group is actually more likely to feel that political parties are doing a good job for the country than the respondents who call

Table 3.3 Attitudes of nonpartisan groups toward political parties (column percents)

	No-preference neither	No-preference leaner	Independent neither	Independent leaner	Partisans
Job rating of political parties					
Good	31.1	26.5	9.2	18.5	24.4
Fair	31.1	40.8	46.0	35.6	41.4
Poor	37.8	32.7	44.8	45.8	34.2
The truth is, we probably don't need political parties in America anymore					
Disagree	35.7	36.5	44.5	47.3	63.5
Pro-con	18.6	14.3	10.0	12.4	10.2
Agree	45.7	49.2	45.5	40.3	26.2
It would be better if in all elections we put no party labels on the ballot					
Disagree	16.7	23.4	29.2	31.0	45.0
Pro-con	19.4	6.3	14.2	11.5	12.2
Agree	63.9	70.3	56.6	57.5	42.8

NOTE: Apoliticals are omitted here because of the small number of cases.
SOURCE: 1980 CPS National Election Study.

themselves Independents. Yet such a finding does not imply that the no-preference group sees parties as relevant in the governmental process; just the opposite seems to be the case. Elsewhere in the 1980 study people were asked whether they agreed or disagreed with the statement, "The truth is we probably don't need political parties in America anymore." On this question the no-preference individuals were actually somewhat less likely to recognize the importance of the parties in the political system by disagreeing with the statement. Similarly, these respondents were also less likely to disagree with the statement, "It would be better if in all elections we put no party labels on the ballot."[11]

They are therefore not so much dissatisfied with the parties as they are unaware of, or ambivalent about, the role they play in the political process. In contrast, respondents who classify themselves as Independents may be largely dissatisfied with the job that the parties are doing, and hence fail to identify with them, but many nevertheless feel that political parties perform a useful function.

The results of this chapter shed new light on the much-discussed decline of party identification in the United States. The proportion of the population labeling themselves as Independents has not risen nearly as much as has previously been thought, while the proportion with no preference has increased steadily over the last several elections. Such a finding has escaped notice in the literature to date because the traditional party identification scale does not provide any distinction between the two types of responses (unless someone with no preference is judged by the election study staff to be so little interested in politics as to warrant being classified as an apolitical).

Of course, if one defines political independence as simply not having a party affiliation, then the distinction is of little value. However, the concept of party identification is based on the premise that party represents a long-standing psychological predisposition that serves as an anchoring point for an individual's political attitudes. The statement that one considers oneself an Independent indicates that one is predisposed not to identify with or be bound to a political party. In contrast, a statement of "no preference" does not indicate any such predisposition.

It has been said that Americans are increasingly becoming turned off and tuned out with respect to political parties. However, the no-preference nonpartisans are evidently not turned off, although they are certainly tuned out. They are alienated in the sense that they lack integration into the party system and that they are less involved in politics than the self-classified Independents. Yet they show less dissatisfaction with the job that the parties are doing and score slightly higher on general measures of system support, such as trust in government, than do Independents. The growth in the proportion of the "no preference" response can be most plausibly interpreted as another indication of the declining salience of political parties in the American political process, which will be the focus of the next several chapters.

4
Negativity or Neutrality?

What has been found thus far about the decline of partisanship in the electorate suggests that political parties are substantially less important to the general public than they were two or three decades ago. Yet much of the literature on party decline in the electorate has postulated disenchantment with the parties as the major causal factor for the decline of partisanship. In *The Changing American Voter,* for example, Norman Nie, Sidney Verba, and John Petrocik argue that voters have come to view the parties in increasingly negative terms.[1]

The two explanations are not, of course, mutually exclusive. One reason the parties are less salient to people could be that they dislike both parties and therefore don't concern themselves much with either. However, it will be argued in this chapter that the increase in dissatisfaction with the parties has been minimal. The major change that has taken place in the public's evaluations of the parties has been that people feel neutral rather than negative. This is not to say that there has not been a decline of partisanship in the electorate, but instead that the nature of the decline has been different from what many have assumed. The distinction is a crucial one for any understanding of the future of American political parties. If voters are actually discontented with political parties, then the parties' chances for recovery in the near future are doubtful; but if people feel only neutral toward them, then the door remains open for party renewal.

Indeed, a good deal of speculation on the future of the political party system rests on the assumption that voters have rejected parties. For example, Kristi Andersen writes that a major difference between the 1920s and the 1970s is that in the twenties those not affiliated with a party were largely apathetic, while in the seventies "there appears to be a more principled rejection of parties." Such a repudiation, she argues, will make the capture of Independents by one of the parties "exceedingly difficult."[2] It is thus crucial to assess whether such a process has in fact been responsible for party decline in the electorate.

An Examination of the Dissatisfaction Hypothesis

The dissatisfaction hypothesis about party decline in the electorate contains two basic components. The first component is the assertion that voters increasingly see no important differences between the Democrats and the Republicans. It has been said that the issues of the 1960s cut across the traditional line of party cleavages and blurred the distinction between the two major parties.[3] As George Wallace said in 1968, "There's not a dime's worth of difference between the two major parties." Second, it has been presumed that because distrust of the government—that is, political cynicism—has risen concurrently with independence, the two trends are related. One of the clearest arguments for the joint impact of these causal factors has been offered by Nie, Verba, and Petrocik. They attribute the increased expressions of disenchantment with the government to the troubles of the late 1960s and proceed to describe the following sequence of events: "The issues of the 1960s ... do not clearly coincide with party lines; thus the parties offer no meaningful alternatives that might tie citizens more closely to them. Thus the political parties reap the results of the disaffection. Citizens come to look at the parties in more negative terms; they also begin to abandon the parties in greater numbers."[4]

The data available from the SRC/CPS election studies do not provide much support for such an interpretation, however. To begin with, as Table 4.1 shows, the proportion of respondents who thought that there were "important differences in what the Republican and Democratic parties stand for"[5] has remained quite stable over the years. Between 1952 and 1976 the proportion seeing important differences fluctuates minimally in the range from

Table 4.1 The electorate's perception of differences in what the two parties stand for

Year	Important differences	No differences, don't know[a]
1952	49.9	50.1
1960	50.3	49.7
1964	50.8	49.2
1968	52.0	48.0
1972	46.1	53.9
1976	47.2	52.8
1980	58.0	42.0

a. In 1964 and 1968 "don't know" was not on the questionnaire; thus the percentage coded as "no difference" was artificially inflated. To make all results comparable, I have combined responses of "no difference" and "don't know."

46 to 52 percent. The data for 1980 show a significant change from 1976, but it is in the opposite direction from what would be predicted by the dissatisfaction hypothesis: in 1980, 58 percent perceived important differences between the parties. It is interesting to note that public perception of party differences was more widespread in 1980 than in either 1964 or 1972, years when, as most scholars would undoubtedly agree, the differences were in reality even sharper.

Nevertheless, the fact that the electorate continues to see important differences in what the parties stand for does not necessarily mean that citizens continue to see the differences as meaning anything in terms of government performance. Since 1960 the election studies have asked respondents what they consider to be the most important problem facing the country. Those who mention a problem are subsequently asked which of the two parties would be the most likely to do what they want on this problem.[6] As can be seen in Table 4.2, the percentage who

Table 4.2 Percent seeing one of the parties as doing the best job on the problem they considered most important

Year	Party mentioned[a]	About the same	Don't know
1960	62.0	25.0	13.0
1964	65.7	25.3	9.0
1968	51.6	38.7[b]	9.8
1972	49.0	42.4	8.6
1976	46.3	46.0	7.7
1980	50.3	42.7	7.1

a. These respondents mentioned either the Democratic or the Republican party.

b. Included are those who saw no difference between the major parties but believed that Wallace would do what they wanted.

SOURCE: SRC/CPS National Election Studies.

feel that one of the parties will do better on the problem that most concerns them has declined since 1964. In that year 65.7 percent thought that one party would be the more likely to do what they wanted, even though only 50.8 percent said that there were important differences in what the parties stood for. In contrast, in 1980 only 50.3 percent thought that one party would be better on the problem they considered most important—which for the first time was significantly lower than the proportion seeing important differences between the parties.

One possible interpretation of this finding is that it represents a growing disenchantment with political parties and the government in general. Merle Black and George Rabinowitz, for instance, note that this pattern bears a striking similarity to trends in trust in government. They write, "If neither party can provide desirable alternative solutions to the problems an individual feels are most important for the government to do something about, it is reasonable for the individual to view the parties unfavorably and lose faith in the government."[7] According to such an interpretation, respondents may still see major differences between the parties but many are so dissatisfied with the opposing alternatives that they have become alienated.

However, those respondents who believe that there wouldn't be any difference between the parties in handling the problem they feel is most important are no more cynical than those who believe that there would be a difference. On a cynicism scale ranging from +100 to −100, the former group is never more than two points more cynical than the latter. In fact, those respondents who feel that there would be no difference between the parties are actually somewhat less cynical in both 1976 and 1980 than their counterparts in these years.

Such a null finding brings into question whether there is any relationship between the respective declines in partisanship and trust in government, as is often presumed. One simple way to establish whether there is such a relationship is to correlate the cynicism scale with strength of party identification. Only in 1968 is there a relationship worth noting. The Pearson correlation between the two variables varies from a high of .11 in 1968 to a low of −.02 in 1972, averaging about .04. It is plausible to infer, therefore, that the initial declines in both party identification and trust in government between 1965 and 1968 were *slightly* intertwined, but there has been no consistent relationship between the two variables.

Yet cross-sectional data can hide systematic changes over time. As Nie et al. emphasize, panel data are necessary for establishing or rejecting a causal link. Fortunately, one panel is now available in which there are substantial declines in both party identification and trust in government—the 1965–1973 Jennings-Niemi socialization panel.[8] This dataset is particularly interesting because it contains a large sample of new entrants into the electorate who have contributed so much to the growth of the nonpartisan group.[9]

If it is true that the decline in party identification is due to the growth of cynicism toward the government, then it would be expected that those in the panel who became more distrusting between 1965 and 1973 would also be the respondents who showed the greatest decline in partisanship. As Table 4.3 demonstrates, however, this was not the case. For example, data on the younger generation (first interviewed as high school seniors in 1965) show that there was a substantial decline in strength of party identification in every cell of the table with very little variation depending on whether the cell represents those

Table 4.3   Change in strength of party identification by change in cynicism toward the government

YOUTH

	1973 cynicism		
	Trusting	In between	Cynical
1965 cynicism			
Trusting	-24.4^a	-36.3	-18.5
(N)	(206)	(307)	(281)
In between	-16.3	-29.4	-22.1
(N)	(49)	(108)	(160)
Cynical	$—^b$	-24.8	-30.2
(N)	(8)	(28)	(63)

PARENTS

	1973 cynicism		
	Trusting	In between	Cynical
1965 cynicism			
Trusting	$-$ 9.9	$+$ 4.3	-13.9
(N)	(153)	(206)	(137)
In between	$+$ 2.1	-12.2	0.0
(N)	(51)	(132)	(157)
Cynical	$—^b$	$-$ 6.1	-17.7
(N)	(16)	(84)	(154)

a. Table entries represent change in strength of party identification from 1965 to 1973. Strength of party identification is calculated by scoring the percentage of Strong Democrats and Strong Republicans as +2, Weak Democrats and Weak Republicans as +1, Independent Democrats and Republicans as 0, and Pure Independents and Apoliticals as 1.

b. Insufficient data.

SOURCE: Jennings-Niemi Socialization Panel Study.

whose cynicism score increased, stayed the same, or decreased. Even the youth who were *least* cynical in both years showed a sizable decline of 24.4 points on strength of partisanship. In comparison, those who shifted from trusting to cynical during the eight-year interval showed only an 18.5 point drop. For the parents the decline in strength of party identification was much smaller, but there is a similar lack of any consistent pattern of changes by cynicism scores. Indeed, some of the cells show changes that are the reverse of what would be expected. The absence of any systematic pattern of changes in the data is best demonstrated by the near-zero correlation between each individual's score on a change in strength of party identification measure (ranging from +3 to −3) and a change in cynicism score (ranging from +5 to −5). These correlations are .01 for the youth cohort and −.01 for the parents.

Thus there is no evidence in this panel to suggest that the rise in cynicism has been responsible for the decline of party identification. It must be concluded that the growth of cynicism and nonpartisanship are roughly parallel trends that have little relationship to each other in both a static and a dynamic sense.

What has been found thus far in this chapter suggests that a reexamination of citizens' attitudes toward the parties is in order. The dissatisfaction hypothesis depends largely on two assumptions—that voters no longer see important differences in what the parties stand for, and that the decline in strength of party identification has been an outgrowth of the decay of public trust in the government—for which little support has been found here.

It is true that there has been a decline in the percentage of the electorate which believes that one party would do a better job in handling whatever they perceive to be the most important governmental problem. However, the fact that such feelings are not related to political distrust indicates that this trend may not necessarily be a reflection of negative attitudes toward the parties. An equally plausible alternative explanation is that citizens simply see the parties as less relevant than in the past, and hence citizens' feelings toward them are more neutral than negative. With the growth of the mass media and candidate-centered campaigns, the importance of parties in the presidential selection process and in government in general has been weakened. The ideological differences between the parties may remain, but on the crucial short-run policy issues of the day it is the candidates that now matter most. Because of these changes there is reason to expect that the electorate should be less positive about the two parties than in the past but that the shift in attitudes will be toward neutrality rather than negativity. Just such a possibility will be examined next.

An Evaluative Perspective on Party Decline

One major weakness in the literature on party decline is that the research has been nearly wholly concerned with the affective (party identification) and behavioral (voting by party line) aspects of the electorate's relationship to political parties. This is not to demean the importance of the decline in strength of party identification and straight-ticket voting; clearly these trends may have significant systemic consequences, most notably the rise in political volatility and instability in the United States. The problem is that such trends have been grafted onto the description of the evaluative dimension of parties as well without proper evidence. That more people choose not to call themselves Democrats or Republicans may not necessarily mean that they are "rejecting" parties, or, as James Sundquist puts it, "calling down a plague on both their houses."[10] Similarly, choosing to split one's ticket also may not imply a long-term rejection of the parties, but rather may simply mean that people no longer view the candidates in partisan terms.

What is sorely lacking is an analysis of just how positive, neutral, or negative Americans are toward the parties and what they like or dislike about them. It is such an evaluative approach that will be presented here. In every presidential election year since 1952 the SRC/CPS election studies have asked respondents in the preelection wave what they liked and disliked about the two political parties. Up to five responses have been coded in each year for each of the four questions.[11] By simply subtracting the number of negative comments from the number of positive ones, respondents can then be classified as either positive, neutral, or negative toward each of the parties, depending on whether the number of likes is greater than, equal to, or less than the number of dislikes.

After collapsing the data into negative, neutral, and positive ratings on each of the two parties, a sixfold classification representing respondents' ratings of both parties was created. The six categories are as follows: (1) *negative-negative,* those who have negative attitudes toward both parties; (2) *negative-neutral,* those who report negative ratings of one party, a neutral evaluation of the other; (3) *neutral-neutral,* those who are neutral with respect to both parties; (4) *positive-negative,* those who report a positive evaluation of one party, a negative evaluation of the other; (5) *positive-neutral,* those who are positive toward one party and neutral toward the other; and (6) *positive-positive,* those who rate both parties in a positive fashion. It should be noted that in all of these categories which party the respondent feels warm, neutral, or cold toward is irrelevant. For example, some of the positive-negative respondents rate the Democrats positively and the Republicans negatively and some vice versa, but what is important here is that these respondents see the parties in a polarized warm-cool fashion, not which party they feel positive toward.

The percentages of respondents falling into the six categories on the basis of these like/dislike questions from 1952 to 1980 are shown in Table 4.4. If it is true that citizens are disenchanted with the parties and have come to perceive them in far more negative terms than in the past, then we would expect to find a large increase in the proportion of negative-negatives and negative-neutrals in the post-1964 period. Certainly this is the case in 1968, the first measurement point available after party identification began to decline. From 1964 to 1968 there is a 5.6 percent increase in those negative toward both parties and a 2.6 percent rise in the negative-neutral category. Given that party identification continued to erode after 1968, it might be hypothesized that the percentage of the electorate with negative attitudes toward the parties would also continue to rise. However, the data clearly shows just the reverse. Between 1968 and 1980 both the negative-negatives and negative-neutrals declined. Thus, the 1968 election stands out as an aberrant year with respect to negative attitudes about the parties, rather than the beginning of a trend.

What does change dramatically after 1968 involves the large increase of the neutral-neutrals and the decline of polarized partisans, that is, the positive-negatives. In 1968 the proportion of polarized partisans was over twice that of the neutral-neutrals; in both 1972 and 1976 the proportion of neutral-neutrals is roughly equal, and in 1980 over 9 percent higher. But what is most fascinating about Table 4.4 is that the increase of those having neutral attitudes to-

Table 4.4 Trends in the public's evaluations of the two major parties

Year	Negative-negative	Negative-neutral	Neutral-neutral	Positive-negative	Positive-neutral	Positive-positive
1952	3.6	9.7	13.0	50.1	18.1	5.5
1956	2.9	9.0	15.9	40.0	23.3	8.9
1960	1.9	7.5	16.8	41.4	24.2	8.3
1964	4.4	11.2	20.2	38.4	20.6	5.0
1968	10.0	13.8	17.3	37.5	17.4	4.1
1972	7.9	12.6	29.9	30.3	14.7	4.7
1976	7.5	11.8	31.3	31.1	13.7	4.5
1980	5.0	8.6	36.5	27.3	17.7	4.8

SOURCE: SRC/CPS National Election Studies.

ward both parties is a trend that is evident throughout the entire twenty-eight-year period—in the "steady state" period as well as in the period of weakening ties to the parties. From 1952 to 1964, while strength of party identification showed little change, the proportion of neutral-neutrals increased with each election, from 13.0 percent in 1952 to 20.2 percent in 1964. Only in 1968 is the linearity of the trend broken because of the largely short-term increase in negativity toward the parties in that year.

It is also evident from the table that the decline of polarized partisans began well before strength of party identification started to drop off. This is especially apparent between 1952 and 1956, when the proportion of positive-negatives fell by over 10 percent. One would intuitively have to hypothesize that the issues of the New Deal, which the party system is generally considered to have been aligned upon, were sharply declining in salience from 1952 to 1956. Through 1960 many of these positive-negatives apparently moved to the less polarized categories of positive-neutral and positive-positive, both of which reached their high points during the years of the Eisenhower presidency. But after 1960 these groups declined in numbers, as did the positive-negatives. Overall, from 1952 to 1980 the percentage of positive-negatives fell from 50.1 to 27.3 percent. Except for the slight increase during the Eisenhower years, the percentage of those positive toward both parties remained fairly stable at about 5 percent.

Given the evidence from Table 4.4, the reader may wonder how Nie, Verba, and Petrocik concluded that citizens had come to look upon parties in more negative terms—especially because they also analyzed responses to the party like/dislike questions.[12] The answer simply is that

Nie et al. combined the categories of negative-negative, negative-neutral, and neutral-neutral into a single group that they labeled variously as "negative evaluations of both parties," "alienated from the parties," or "nonsupporters of the parties." Only the third phrase is an accurate description of what they were measuring. To infer that a neutral evaluation of the parties represents dissatisfaction is to make an extremely tenuous assumption, especially since the growth of neutrality on these open-ended questions has been entirely due to the increase (from 9.7 to 34.3 percent) in the proportion of the population who have nothing at all to say—either positive or negative—about either party, and hence end up being classified as neutral toward both.[13]

Additional Evidence from Feeling Thermometers

Another point that Nie et al. make about the increase in negative attitudes concerns the decline over time in the public's feeling thermometer ratings of the parties. As shown in Figure 4.1, the mean rating of "Democrats" has fallen by about eight points since 1964, and the mean rating of "Republicans" shortly after the Reagan victory in 1980 was actually lower than during the Goldwater debacle in 1964.

But do lower ratings necessarily indicate the presence of more intense negative evaluations? Because feeling thermometer ratings represent a summary of both positive and negative affect, the trends shown in Figure 4.1 could just as easily be due to a decline in positive feelings as to a rise in negative ones. Furthermore, it is quite possible that if *both* positive and negative feelings were to decline in intensity, the net result would be a lower mean

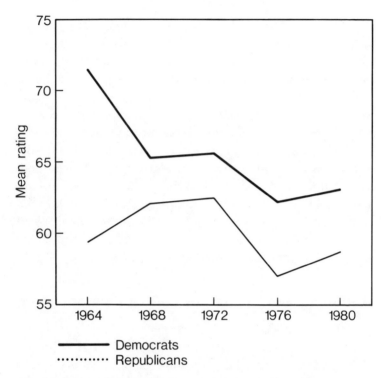

Figure 4.1   Feeling thermometer ratings of the parties, 1964–1980
Source: SRC/CPS National Election Studies.

rating. This is because of the positivity bias that is usually associated with the feeling thermometer instrument. For example, on the like/dislike measure one never finds more than 9 percent of the population giving a positive evaluation of both parties (see Table 4.4), while an average of nearly 40 percent rate both parties at above the neutral point—that is, 50 degrees—on the feeling thermometer. Thus one could find people who are positive as well as those who are negative gravitating equally toward the neutral point, but the fact that the distributions are so heavily skewed toward the positive side means that there will be more downward than upward movement.

From Table 4.5 we can see that such a decline in the intensity of *both* positive and negative feelings toward the parties has in fact taken place. Those who give favorable ratings now give less favorable ones than in the past. Similarly, respondents who give negative ratings are now less intensely negative than in the mid-1960s. These trends are best summarized by taking the absolute value of the distance of the ratings from 50 degrees. In 1964 the average respondent evaluated the two parties such that the combined distance of both ratings from the neutral point was 46.1 points (26.5 for ratings of "Democrats" plus 19.6 for ratings of "Republicans").[14] By 1976 the comparable figure

Table 4.5 Trends in the intensity of feeling thermometer ratings of the parties

	1964	1968	1972	1976	1980
Rating of "Democrats"					
Average distance above 50 degrees for those positive	34.0	29.9	26.2	24.4	25.5
Average distance below 50 degrees for those negative	24.0	22.5	17.1	17.0	18.1
Average distance from 50 degrees (includes those at 50)	26.5	21.3	19.1	15.5	17.5
Rating of "Republicans"					
Average distance above 50 degrees for those positive	28.4	27.2	25.1	21.6	21.8
Average distance below 50 degrees for those negative	26.5	25.1	22.7	19.7	20.6
Average distance from 50 degrees (includes those at 50)	19.6	18.9	18.2	12.7	14.6

SOURCE: SRC/CPS National Election Studies.

had fallen by nearly 40 percent to 28.2. There is a slight increase between 1976 and 1980 in the intensity of feeling thermometer ratings of the parties, but it hardly represents a major reversal of the trend.[15] The overall picture is clearly one of movement toward the neutral point from both the positive and negative sides of the scale.

In sum, the results from both the like/dislike responses and the feeling thermometers reinforce one another despite their methodological differences. In each the major trend is a growing neutrality in the electorate's perception of the parties. The fact that similar trends can be found with disparate sets of data provides a pleasing confirmation of the theoretical framework outlined above.

A Comparison of Party Images in 1952 and 1980

Just how fragile the current party alignment has become because of the rise in neutrality can be illustrated by the lack of substance in respondents' party images, as revealed in the 1980 election study. As Table 4.6 demonstrates, the only major advantage enjoyed by either party is the positive image of the groups that the Democrats are perceived as representing. Similarly, the only major disadvantage for either party is the negative image that people have of the groups popularly associated with the Republican Party. These feelings that the Democrats are the party of the common working man while the Republicans are the party of the upper class and big business represent virtually the last remnant of the images of the parties that developed during the New Deal era.

Table 4.7 presents an examination of the party images found in the 1952 election study, which can be directly compared to the percentages displayed in Table 4.6 for

Table 4.6 Images of the political parties, 1980

	Like Democrats	Dislike Democrats	Like Republicans	Dislike Republicans
Because of:				
The groups they are for or against	25.5	4.2	4.3	19.3
Economic/welfare policy stands	6.2	10.0	8.1	3.9
Social issue stands	0.8	0.7	1.0	1.1
Stands on general philosophy of government activity	8.1	8.2	11.1	5.1
Their ability to manage the government	2.5	9.7	7.2	2.0
Foreign policy	4.2	6.3	7.4	4.5
Carter	0.6	1.9	—	—
Reagan	—	—	1.1	1.5

NOTE: Table entries are the proportion of the sample offering each given type of response.
SOURCE: 1980 CPS National Election Study.

Table 4.7 Images of the political parties, 1952

Because of:	Like Democrats	Dislike Democrats	Like Republicans	Dislike Republicans
The groups they are for or against	33.1	4.7	3.2	20.3
Economic/welfare policy stands	31.9	16.3	22.1	22.4
Social issue stands	—	—	—	—
Stands on general philosophy of government activity	11.4	8.7	11.0	5.8
Their ability to manage the government	2.3	26.6	18.0	4.3
Foreign policy	4.1	17.1	12.3	3.4
Truman	1.0	7.6	—	—
Eisenhower	—	—	7.7	1.8
Stevenson	1.3	0.9	—	—

SOURCE: 1952 SRC National Election Study.

1980. The comparison indicates that there has been a marked deterioration of images that once were highly favorable to the Democrats and of those that once greatly benefited the Republicans. Leaving aside the long-standing impressions of which parties favor which groups, the electorate just no longer has much to say when asked what they like and dislike about the two parties.

In 1952, for example, nearly a third of the respondents stated that they liked the Democratic Party because of its economic or welfare policies, while 22 percent made negative comments along those lines in reference to the Republicans. With memories of the Depression now in the distant past, it is probably not too surprising to find that the comparable figures in 1980 were only 6 and 4 percent, respectively. Many observers may be surprised to find, however, that positive comments about the Republican Party's economic/welfare policy stands were also more numerous in the 1952 sample than in 1980 (22 percent compared to 8 percent). Moreover, despite the poor performance of the economy during the Carter administration, only 10 percent of those interviewed made negative comments about the economic and welfare policies of the Democratic Party. In sum, neither party now has a very firmly entrenched positive or negative public image on such issues compared to two or three decades ago.[16]

In the areas of foreign policy and management of the government, the images of the parties are also not nearly as clearly defined as they once were. In both 1952 and 1980 the Republicans were perceived favorably on these dimensions while the Democrats were viewed negatively because of dissatisfaction with the performances of Truman and Carter, respectively. The key difference to note is that in 1980 such feelings were far less salient than in

1952. The fact that only 7 percent of those interviewed made positive comments about the Republicans on each of these dimensions in 1980 hardly constitutes a resounding statement of faith in Republican foreign policies or management capabilities. Nor is there any indication that Carter's failures in these areas are likely to have a long-term negative impact on the Democratic Party, as the comparable negative figures in 1952 were nearly three times as high.

That the Democratic Party largely escaped blame for the entire range of problems of the Carter administration, from the economy to Iran, might be interpreted as an incredible stroke of good fortune, especially considering that such problems were quite prevalent in open-ended evaluations of Jimmy Carter in 1980. However, such a pattern is more likely a symptom of the dissociation of public perceptions of candidates and presidents from the political parties that they nominally represent. With the rise of the plebiscitary presidency and the growth of the mass media, candidates no longer need the parties to convey their messages and voters are now able to see for themselves just what the candidates are like. A number of recent presidential campaigns—most notably that of Richard Nixon in 1972—have thus been able to consciously downplay partisan appeals.

In 1980 neither candidate really made any effort to avoid party associations, however. Reagan clearly attempted to be more of a Republican team man than any nominee in the party's recent history, and Carter stressed his Democratic affiliation to the utmost given that his low approval ratings made it difficult to offer much else in the way of a positive appeal. In spite of these strategies, very few people evaluated the parties in 1980 on the basis of their standard-bearers, as shown in Table 4.6. For example, only 1 percent of the sample stated that they liked the Republicans because of Ronald Reagan. Whether this figure will be much greater in the future if the Reagan program succeeds remains to be seen, but if so it would mark a reversal of the historical trend that will be the major focus of the following chapter. In this candidate-centered media age, people have apparently become less accustomed to praising or blaming the parties for presidential performance.

The results presented in this chapter offer somewhat more hope for the revitalization of American political parties than most previous work on the subject. However, one can also extrapolate reasons to be doubtful about such a prospect, based on the interpretation of party decline that has been argued here.

Taking the positive side first, the most important new piece of data is that there has been little increase in the proportion of the population holding negative attitudes toward the parties. It is conceivable that the initial decline in strength of party identification may have been due to the large jump in negativity apparent in 1968. But since that time negative attitudes toward the parties have subsided. Positive attitudes have also continued to decline, but what has increased has been neutrality rather than negativity.

Besides the fact that parties do not have to overcome largely negative attitudes toward them, it is also encouraging to note that their recovery probably does not hinge on a restoration of trust in government. Like other institutions, political parties are viewed more cynically than in the past. However, this sort of cynicism is apparently not being translated into negative attitudes. People may be more skeptical about the motives of parties, but that does not necessarily mean that they dislike parties in general or that they will not identify with a party in the future. This point is supported by the fact that hardly any relationship was found between strength of party identification and trust in government, except for the .11 correlation in 1968. And in a dynamic sense, panel data show that the two trends are quite independent of one another. Given that the decline of partisanship has been a reflection of growing neutrality instead of negativity, such null findings are quite explicable. If negative attitudes about parties were at the root of the rise of nonpartisanship then one would expect that other negative attitudes such as cynicism would be related to it, as indeed the case of 1968 appears to show. But overall the evidence demonstrates that the decline of parties in the electorate has been more a function of a reduction in saliency than an increase in negative attitudes.

However, turning to the reasons to be pessimistic about any revitalization of parties in the electorate, there seems to be little prospect for reversing the trend toward neutrality in the immediate future. One of the most important findings in this chapter is that the decline of parties in the electorate can be traced back much further than the mid-1960s in terms of party evaluations. The decline of polarized views of the parties and the increase in neutrality is visible throughout the election study time series. Thus it can undoubtedly be considered a long-term secular trend, and such trends are usually difficult to reverse.

5
Political Leadership and the Parties

The analytical problem, as defined by the growth in neutrality described in the preceding chapter, is to explain why political parties are now less important to the public than in the past. It will be helpful, therefore, to consider what elements of the political world influence the salience of concepts such as partisanship in the first place. A useful starting point can be found in the chapter on membership in social groupings in *The American Voter*. Campbell, Converse, Miller, and Stokes write:

Political salience . . . refers to any heightening of awareness of a particular group membership at the time when the individual is oriented to the political world. This dimension . . . is especially subject to short-term variation, since salience usually depends on the most transient objects of political orientation: the candidates and the issues.

Political salience of the group is high, for example, when a candidate for the election is recognized as a member of the group.[1]

In other words, without candidates and issues with which political parties can be identified, the salience of partisanship in the electorate is likely to suffer. The key variable is of course leadership, for the link between issues and parties depends heavily on the candidate's actions, that is, his or her treatment of issues in partisan terms—stressing that as a Democrat or a Republican he or she stands for certain ideas and policies. It is thus crucial to note that for a variety of institutional reasons candidates now have substantially less incentive to foster the link between themselves and the parties, as well as between political issues and the parties. As Lester Seligman has written, "Deprived of presidential support, political parties are losing their meaning to the voters. Increasingly, Presidents are no longer making political parties and parties are no longer making Presidents."[2]

At the outset of this book it was noted that recruiting and nominating candidates is one of the functions that political parties are called on to perform. In fact, back in the days when parties still played a central role in selecting presidential candidates, E. E. Schattschneider singled out this function as perhaps the most crucial of all. "Unless the party makes authoritative and effective nominations, it cannot stay in business," wrote Schattschneider. "The nature of the nominating procedure determines the nature of the party."[3] More recently, former Congressman Donald Fraser has taken a similar point of view. He writes, "To the extent that the organized party abdicates responsibility for the selection of its candidates, it becomes almost irrelevant to the solution of the problems facing our nation."[4]

The deterioration of the traditional role of parties in the presidential selection process has been thoroughly documented in the literature and need not be reviewed in detail for our purposes.[5] Basically, the crux of the change has been to alter the constituency on which candidates are dependent for nomination from the party organization regulars to the public at large and the mass media.

At first, the strategy of conducting a candidate-centered media campaign to develop a candidate's popular appeal was effective largely to the extent to which it fostered support among the party leaders. For example, John F. Kennedy's victories in several key Democratic primaries in 1960 were an important factor in his nomination, but without the support he gathered from the party leaders he would in all likelihood have met the same fate as Estes Kefauver—who won twelve of thirteen primaries in 1952 yet lost the nomination fight as a direct result of opposition from the party leadership.[6]

Since 1968, however, the proportion of convention delegates selected via primary elections has risen from about one-third to four-fifths, thereby making the accumulation of primary votes the key to nomination. In addition, the delegates selected in caucuses are no longer as organizationally oriented as in the past, for the caucus process has been substantially opened in order to forestall leadership manipulation. Comparing primary and caucus-selected delegates, Barbara Farah finds virtually no differences between the two in terms of orientation to party or representativeness.[7] Indeed, it is the open caucus in Iowa, as much as the New Hampshire and other early primaries, which now performs the function of narrowing down the presidential field. Those candidates who fare poorly in Iowa, New Hampshire, and the other early contests receive only minimal attention in the media and are soon written off as serious contenders.[8] Where once the organizational leaders played the role of talent scouts and assessors based on past performance in governing, reporters now do so based on performance in caucuses and primaries.

The net result of the many changes in the nomination process has led Austin Ranney to dub the new process aptly as "closely approaching a no-party system." His summary of the current state of affairs is instructive and worth quoting at length:

Presidential nominations are contested by candidate-centered organizations. Each organization is assembled by the candidate and his inner circle. Each is financed in part by funds it raises and in part by federal matching funds . . . Each appeals to the party rank and file in primaries, caucuses, and conventions with little concern for what the state organizational leaders do or don't do. The party organizations simply are not actors in presidential politics. Indeed, they are little more than custodians of the party-label prize which goes to the winning candidate organization. The parties have long since ceased to be judges *awarding* the prize.[9]

Not only do parties—as institutions—now play a greatly reduced role in nominating and electing the president, they also have been pushed out of the public spotlight in terms of actual governing. Presidents have always had a tendency to try to bypass parties once in office by appealing to the national interest and to the people as a whole, but the growth of the Executive branch has made such a strategy eminently more feasible and rewarding. Since the start of the New Deal the number of White House aides has grown from about the size of the Supreme Court to that of the U.S. Congress. More than one hundred of these aides are now involved in some form of public relations, according to Cronin—"busily selling and reselling the President."[10] Furthermore, there are presidential assistants to deal with virtually every major policy area and to build lines of support with virtually all existing interest groups. As Hugh Heclo has written, "If one were inventing a political party, these are exactly the types of offices at branch headquarters that one would want to create. What is lacking is only the local cells that would give such an organization feet and hands."[11]

Turning to the congressional level, changes have also occurred so as to make the public less likely to link parties with candidates and issues. Here, there is empirical evidence indicating that members of Congress are increasingly acting in a less partisan manner. As Figure 5.1 shows, the percentage of party-line votes cast in the House of Representatives has steadily fallen from one administration to the next. During the years when Franklin Roosevelt was in office the majority of Democrats voted in opposition to the majority of Republicans on nearly 60 percent of all the recorded roll calls; by the Nixon-Ford years this figure had dropped to under 35 percent. A small increase in party-line voting did occur in Carter's term, but in part this may just be a reflection of the fact that the Democrats once again controlled both the presidency and Congress, as divided control tends to foster somewhat less partisan behavior.

Of course, it would be out of the question to assume that the mass public is really very aware of this decline in party voting in Congress. However, the public is exposed to the new style of congressional campaigning—a style that fits in nicely with this quantitative evidence of increasingly less partisan behavior once elected to office. As Fiorina has argued, the growth of the Washington bureaucratic establishment has enabled members of Congress to

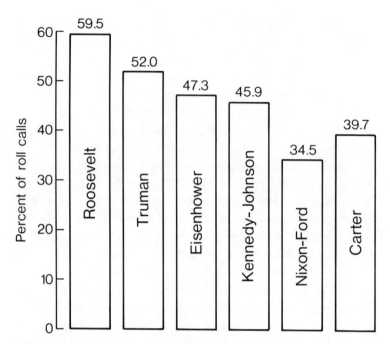

Figure 5.1 Party-line voting in the House from Roosevelt to Carter

Note: Percentages shown represent averages for the Congresses during each administration or combination of administrations.

Sources: Data for 1932–1976 taken from David W. Brady and Charles S. Bullock III, "Coalition Politics in the House of Representatives," in Lawrence C. Dodd and Bruce I. Oppenheimer, eds., *Congress Reconsidered*, 2d ed. (Washington, D.C.: Congressional Quarterly Press, 1981). Percentage for the Carter administration calculated by the author from *Congressional Quarterly Reports* for these years.

run for office as ombudsmen, assisting constituents with problems with the federal government and bringing home pork-barrel projects for the district.[12] Such activities are noncontroversial, and hence can only aid one's reelection. More important, they are also nonpartisan. The result, no doubt, is that many voters have come to feel that if their representative is doing a good job helping out people in the district then it shouldn't matter whether he or she is a Democrat or a Republican.

Public Evaluations of Parties and Candidates

To investigate whether these changes have in fact been reflected by a change in the public's evaluations of the relationship between parties and candidates, we need to examine comparable time series data concerning each from the election studies. Such data are available in the form of the traditional open-ended questions, which ask respondents what they like and dislike about the two parties and whether there is anything in particular that might make them vote for or against the two major presidential candidates. As utilized elsewhere in this work, counting the number of positive responses and then subtracting the number of negative ones yields a summary score of net affect toward each party and candidate. And as Figure 5.2 demonstrates, the correlation between party and candidate evaluations has indeed declined over the years. The correlation between ratings of Carter and the Democratic Party in 1980 represents the weakest relationship between public perceptions of a candidate and his party in the historical time series, and on the Republican side only ratings of Gerald Ford were less related to Republican Party evaluations than those of Ronald Reagan. Most revealing of all, however, is the secular decline in the correlation between the partisan direction (that is, affect toward Democrats minus affect toward Republicans) of candidate and party evaluations from .70 in 1952 to .54 in 1980—or, in terms of common variance, from 49 to 29 percent.

In part, this change is probably attributable to the fact

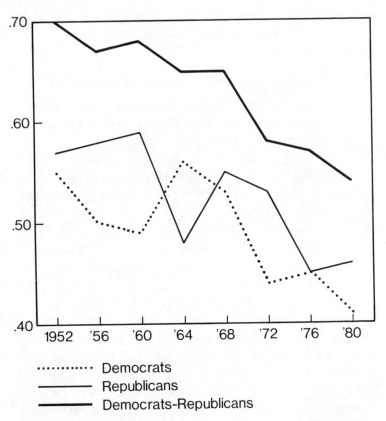

.... Democrats
————— Republicans
━━━━━ Democrats-Republicans

Figure 5.2 Correlations between party and candidate like/ dislike measures, 1952–1980
Source: SRC/CPS National Election Studies.

that spontaneous references to party affiliation in response to the candidate questions have declined substantially over the years.[13] For example, 15.7 percent of those interviewed in 1952 said that they either liked or disliked Stevenson because he was a Democrat and 9.5 percent expressed a like or dislike of Eisenhower because he was a Republican. By comparison, only 2.9 percent mentioned Carter's party affiliation in 1980 and 4.1 percent mentioned Reagan's.

But *why* are parties and candidates less tightly linked in public perceptions than in the past? Theoretically, what should bind the two together is a commonality in issue stands. Knowing a candidate's party affiliation alone should give the citizen an issue basis for evaluation of the candidate. Under such a framework issues are largely partisan matters which get translated at election time into assessments of candidates, rather than being transient concerns which are primarily candidate-centered. Given the historical changes discussed above, however, there is good reason to believe that the latter pattern may well have become more prevalent than the former.

It will be recalled from Chapter 4 that when respondents are asked which major party would do best in solving whatever they consider to be the most important problem of the day, an increasing proportion have been responding that there would be no difference. This trend cannot be explained by an increase in the perception that there are no longer important differences between the parties, for there has not been any such increase. Nor can it be attributed to the decline in trust in government. Thus it might be hypothesized that more citizens are now conceptualizing issues in terms of candidates only and less in terms of party alone. In other words, the stands that candidates take on the issues may no longer be linked to voters' perceptions of the parties. The parties may still stand for certain broad principles and groups, but when it comes to specific policies, candidates now stand *above* parties rather than with them.

To test this hypothesis, we can compare the frequency

of responses to the candidate like/dislike questions to the frequency of likes and dislikes expressed about the parties on four substantive dimensions or response categories: domestic issues, foreign issues, benefits provided to groups, and general political philosophy.[14] If such a hypothesis is correct, then one would expect an increase over time in the proportion of the population commenting about issues with respect to the candidates but not with respect to parties. Such a pattern would indicate that issues are irrelevant to the citizen in evaluating parties but relevant with regard to the candidates.

Table 5.1 provides evidence that such a pattern has become much more prevalent over the years, especially on domestic and foreign policy. For example, domestic issues were overwhelmingly associated with the parties in 1952, with only 2.7 percent making such comments with reference only to candidates, compared to 53.5 percent for parties only. But by 1964 the balance had shifted dramatically to the point where more respondents were mentioning domestic issues only in terms of candidates than parties only, and in 1980 the ratio is over two to one in favor of the candidate-only response pattern. References to parties and candidates on foreign policy were roughly balanced in 1952, but the same trend is nevertheless apparent. By 1964 the percentage in the candidate-only category was twice that of the party-only group, and in 1980 41.6 percent of the sample mentioned foreign policy in reference to a candidate but not with respect to either party, while only 3.5 percent displayed the reverse pattern. Finally, while there is a slight decrease in the party-only response pattern for the dimensions of group benefits and general philosophy of government, these attitudes still remain predominantly the domain of the parties, and thus probably account for the lack of any drop in the percentage of the population perceiving major differences between the parties.

One particularly interesting feature of these data is that because they are based on preelection information, they refer in large part to the politics of the previous four years and are usually influenced only in minor part by nonincumbent candidacies. Thus the 1952 data can be seen as capturing the perceived importance of parties over candidates that had developed by the last of the New Deal administrations, and the change that occurred between 1952 and 1956 suggests the extent to which the Eisenhower presidency diminished the salience of party on domestic and foreign issues. Eisenhower's distrust of partisanship and his "above party" stance were well known and undoubtedly had a major effect on the public's conceptualization of the issues. As he himself stated during a 1954 press conference: "I think it is quite apparent that I am not very much of a partisan. The times are too serious, I think, to indulge in partisanship to the extreme."[15] The virtual identicalness of the 1956 and 1960 figures reflect quite properly that the perceptions put into place by the first four years of the Eisenhower presidency simply persisted over the next four. Between 1960 and 1964, however, the most dramatic four-year change can be seen on domestic issues, in part due to Goldwater's extraordinarily issue-oriented campaign but also indicating that after four years of the Kennedy-Johnson administrations the linking of domestic issues with party had been dealt another severe blow. Strong leadership overshadowed the parties and hence issues became further personified. Goldwater's disappearance from the national scene and the partisan controversy stirred by the implementation of

Table 5.1 The frequency of substantive responses to the party and candidate like/dislike questions

	Mentioned for neither	Mentioned for party only	Mentioned for candidate only	Mentioned for both
Domestic issues				
1952	36.7	53.5	2.7	7.1
1956	49.9	31.8	7.8	10.4
1960	51.7	31.0	7.2	10.1
1964	46.8	15.9	20.5	16.7
1968	54.1	22.0	11.2	12.7
1972	49.6	14.2	21.6	14.7
1976	50.9	19.8	16.6	12.7
1980	46.6	11.0	27.7	14.7
Foreign issues				
1952	55.6	17.4	16.2	10.8
1956	59.9	12.1	16.8	11.2
1960	56.9	13.1	18.8	11.1
1964	64.3	9.0	19.5	7.2
1968	54.7	13.9	20.0	11.4
1972	46.1	6.6	39.1	8.2
1976	74.3	9.1	11.5	5.1
1980	46.0	3.5	41.6	8.8

Benefits provided to groups

1952	54.0	33.2	4.7	8.1
1956	51.1	32.7	5.3	10.9
1960	56.8	28.3	4.3	10.6
1964	54.4	27.2	7.4	10.9
1968	58.5	25.4	5.5	10.6
1972	54.7	23.8	8.5	12.9
1976	55.0	24.3	9.1	11.6
1980	59.7	28.3	5.2	6.9

General political philosophy

1952	65.1	20.9	8.8	5.2
1956	76.3	15.7	4.9	3.1
1960	68.1	15.9	9.5	6.5
1964	54.6	14.8	16.5	14.1
1968	54.2	19.3	13.7	12.7
1972	62.8	16.7	12.3	8.2
1976	63.6	17.8	10.9	7.7
1980	69.7	13.2	9.1	7.9

Source: SRC/CPS National Election Studies.

Johnson's Great Society program produced a significant resurgence of party on domestic issues in 1968, but by 1972 Nixon's "imperial presidency" and the disarray of the Democrats pushed the relative salience of party on domestic policy to yet another new low. In addition, Nixon's strong personal handling of foreign policy and McGovern's extreme stance on Vietnam resulted in the largest four-year decline in the relative salience of parties versus candidates on foreign issues. Once again in 1976 we see some regression back to the previous state of affairs, probably because of the relative dearth of public knowledge about the issue stands of both Ford and Carter in that year. However, the most recent data from 1980 show a further continuation of the trend toward pure candidate orientation in the public's conceptualization of both domestic and foreign issues. The 1980 election focused primarily on the relative abilities of the candidates to handle successfully the problems of inflation, unemployment, and the hostage crisis in Iran,[16] and therefore it should not be surprising to find that the public came to view the issues in a more candidate-centered fashion than ever before.

Thus it seems clear that political leadership is one crucial variable in determining why the electorate has become more neutral toward the political parties. As presidential candidates have increasingly come to assume a much larger share of the spotlight on domestic and foreign policy, the parties have seen much of their base of support erode. A contest for the electorate's attention has taken place throughout the 1952–1980 period between presidential candidates and political parties, and a series of strong candidates have all contributed to the erosion of the electoral salience of parties. The likes and dislikes that citizens perceive for leaders on the issues are apparently not being translated into similar attitudes toward the parties.

Finally, in an attempt to advance, and further clarify, the argument that leadership is one of the key reasons behind the rise in neutrality, we can also examine responses concerning leaders on the *party* like/dislike questions. If the explanation for party decline is simply that candidates have become more salient, then one might expect that more people would be referring to leaders when asked about their likes and dislikes of the parties, even though other types of responses on the open-ended party questions have decreased. But if the decline is also due to the fact that the link between parties and candidates has been weakened, then it is probable that fewer people would be mentioning leaders when probed for their opinions about the parties, despite the fact that candidates have become increasingly salient to the electorate.

In working with these responses, one must be careful to compare years in which the leadership situations were as similar as possible; otherwise the results might simply be due to some exogenous factor such as whether the incumbent was running for reelection or not. The best set of comparisons that can be made are those between 1956 and 1972, when a popular incumbent was seeking reelection, and between 1964 and 1976, when recent mid-term successors to the presidential office sought a term of their own.

These two comparisons support the hypothesis that the party-candidate link has indeed deteriorated. In 1956, 34.4 percent of the respondents mentioned a party figure as a reason for liking or disliking a party; only 19.0 percent did so in 1972. The comparable figures for 1964 and 1976 are

20.4 and 14.5 percent, respectively. The first comparison is particularly interesting, for Eisenhower was a far less partisan figure than Nixon. One plausible explanation could be Eisenhower's great personal popularity in 1956. Yet it is not merely positive responses about party leaders that were more prevalent in 1956; dislikes were more frequently mentioned as well. In fact, more people, when asked what they disliked about the Democratic Party, mentioned party leaders in 1956 than in 1972, even though Stevenson was a far more popular standard-bearer than McGovern. Regarding the incumbent party, 9.4 percent expressed some dislike of its leaders in 1956 compared to only 3.4 percent in 1972. Although most of the negative comments concerning the Republicans in 1956 were directed at Nixon rather than Eisenhower, it is somewhat unexpected that fewer people would give similar comments about him in 1972, when he was an incumbent president.

At least a partial answer to the question "Why the growing neutrality toward the parties?" seems to be that fewer people are translating their likes and dislikes about the candidates and the candidates' stands on specific issues into likes and dislikes about the parties. Thus the appearance of a major realigning issue—which is so often considered to be the best hope for reviving the parties—may not have any strengthening effect on partisanship in the electorate. The reason for party decline has not been that people no longer see any important differences between the parties. Indeed, the trend toward neutrality would have been even sharper if the frequency of comments concerning the general philosophies and group benefits offered by the parties had not remained fairly stable. Rather, the problem the parties face is that they are considered less relevant in solving the most important domestic and foreign policy issues of the day. In the voters' minds, the parties are losing their association with the candidates and the issues that the candidates claim to stand for. Therefore, major new issues that arise will probably not help the parties rebuild their base of support unless voters are convinced that the parties can serve a meaningful function that candidates alone cannot.

6
The Role of the Media

Thus far it has been argued that the decline of partisanship has involved a change in the public agenda from parties to candidates. Naturally, any time such an agenda change is found it must be considered what part the media has played—for its role in shaping the public agenda is well known.

The tremendous growth of the media has undoubtedly been one of the most important factors in reshaping the American electoral scene in recent years. Where once candidates for public office had to rely on mustering organizational strength to communicate with voters, it is now increasingly possible for them to establish direct contact through the media. As a result, what Robert Agranoff has labeled "the candidate-centered campaign" has come into prominence.[1] Once, a major theme of most campaigns involved stressing the candidate's party affiliation; now candidates often run campaigns that de-emphasize party ties whenever possible. As Fiorina has written, "Candidates would have little incentive to operate campaigns independent of parties if there were no means to apprise the citizenry of their independence.

The media provide the means" (emphasis mine).[2] There is of course nothing inherent about the media which requires that campaigns be run independently of party; rather, the growth of the media has simply made this strategy far more feasible. Such a style of media campaigning reinforces attitudes about candidates but does little to reinforce partisan attitudes. As Frank Sorauf writes, "It is the candidate, not the party, who is 'sold.' The image transmitted by TV and the other media is of a person, not of the abstraction known as a political party."[3]

Newspaper and television reporting have in all likelihood also fostered the declining salience of political parties. Newspapers, which were once one of the prime reinforcers of partisanship, now take a largely independent line—especially in the everyday reporting of the news. As James Sundquist has noted, it is rare today to find a newspaper which endorses a straight party slate: "A self-respecting editor feels obliged to advise his readers to split their tickets."[4] And television coverage of politics virtually ignores parties, as acquaintance with personalities is much easier to convey through the visual media than knowledge about abstractions such as political parties.

Despite the frequent assertions in the literature of the media's contribution to the decline of partisanship, the evidence has remained almost entirely impressionistic. The goal of this chapter is to remedy this deficiency by first examining data that demonstrate the historical shift in the focus of election coverage from parties to candidates, and then analyzing the effects of candidate media advertising on the salience of partisan attitudes in the mass public.

A Content Analysis of Election Coverage

Are political parties in fact now receiving less coverage in election reporting, compared to candidates, than in the past? With the great number of media sources in the United States, attempting to reach a definitive empirical answer to this question would require resources far beyond those available for this inquiry. However, I sought to test this hypothesis on a limited basis by examining the content of election coverage between 1952 and 1980 in two major metropolitan newspapers and three national weekly news magazines. The two newspapers—the *Chicago Tribune* and the *Washington Post*—were selected randomly from a rather limited selection; no claim can be made for their being representative of the cross-section of newspapers around the country. The selection of the three weekly news magazines—*Newsweek, Time,* and *U.S. News and World Report*—was somewhat less arbitrary, as they constitute the only major national weekly news magazines published throughout this period.

The research design employed was to have students code a portion of the election coverage for each presidential election from 1952 to 1980, dividing up the workload so that each student coded roughly the same amount of material in each year.[5] All election-related stories in September and October were coded for each news source, totaling 10,115 stories in all over the course of eight elections. The major objective of the coding was to count the number of times political parties were mentioned by name in the stories and headlines compared to presidential candidates. In addition, on a more subjective level, coders were instructed to look for and count the number of substantive linkages between parties and candidates in the content of the stories.

Starting with the results from coding the stories, the data clearly indicate that media coverage of candidates has increasingly come to dominate that of parties in the newspapers and magazines selected for analysis.[6] Although the total number of campaign-related stories declined in this period, the actual number of mentions of presidential candidates per year stayed relatively stable. In contrast, the number of instances in which parties were mentioned by name in the stories fell precipitously. More theoretically important than the raw count of mentions, however, is the ratio between coverage of candidates versus that of parties, as this focuses attention squarely on the question of the *relative* degree to which the reading audience was exposed to candidates versus parties. Throughout the whole 1952–1980 period, mentions of candidates outnumbered those of parties, but as Figure 6.1 shows, the ratio increased from about two to one in the 1950s to roughly five to one by 1980. In short, it is clear that subscribers to these newspapers and magazines have over the years been increasingly exposed to a candidate-centered view of presidential campaigns.

A similar finding can be shown for the appearance of candidates and parties in the headlines of election coverage. A headline is an important barometer of what editors feel is most important in the news, as it is used to draw attention to a story and single out its key points. And as Figure 6.2 demonstrates, the editors for these news sources have increasingly come to believe that candidates are more newsworthy, and therefore more appropriate as headline material, than political parties. Given that there is much less material to code in headlines than in stories, it should not be surprising to find a somewhat less linear trend in the candidate/party ratio for the former. There is little doubt nevertheless that headline writers are much

Figure 6.1 Ratio of mentions of candidates to parties in stories, 1952–1980

less inclined than in the past to place political parties in bold print, where even the most casual reader might take notice.

Beyond the straightforward counting of mentions of parties and candidates in election stories and headlines it

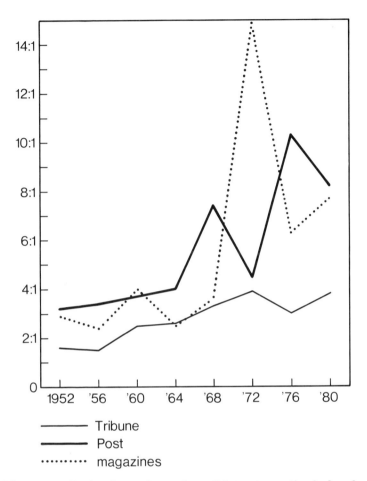

Tribune
Post
magazines

Figure 6.2   Ratio of mentions of candidates to parties in head-lines, 1952–1980

is also important to examine some of the substance of election reporting. In particular, the data concerning the increased separation between public attitudes toward parties and candidates documented in the previous chapter would lead us to hypothesize that the party-candidate linkage is one theme that may be far less prevalent in election reporting than in the past.

Coders were thus instructed to count the number of instances in which presidential candidates were in some way tied to their party. This could be done in an election story by the reporter, by one of the candidates themselves, or by some other political figure. An example of the first kind of linkage would be a story reading, "Ronald Reagan campaigned in the Northeast yesterday expressing the usual Republican philosophy of free enterprise to traditional Republican constituencies." The second type would be exemplified by a quotation of Reagan saying, "Jimmy Carter favors the old Democratic beliefs of big spending and represents a party whose ideas have failed the test of time." (Note that in this case the linkage is the result of one candidate's linking his opponent to the opposition party.) And finally, if some other political figure was quoted as making such a statement (for instance, Truman in 1952 or Ford in 1980), then it was coded under the third type of substantive linkage.

The *total* number of linkages per year in each news source is displayed graphically in Figure 6.3, indicating a decline in magnitude of approximately two-thirds from 1952 to 1980.[7] If these linkages are broken down into the three categories described above, the trends are found to be remarkably similar. Candidates and other political figures are being quoted less often as making partisan statements and reporters are not invoking the theme of linkage between party and candidate as often as in the past. Whether all of this is due to changes in candidate behavior, or, alternatively, to changes in political reporting, is impossible to determine for certain. The degree to which this trend can be attributed to the reporters and editors is questionable, as it is difficult to say whether they are se-

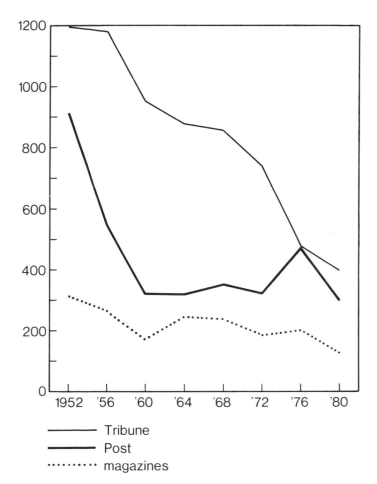

Figure 6.3 Number of substantive linkages between parties and candidates, 1952–1980

lectively reporting or mirroring the themes of the campaign. However, considering the sharpness of the decline, it seems unlikely that such linkages would be appearing so much less often in print if candidates were still emphasizing partisanship as frequently as in the past.

It has been found, then, that political parties have been increasingly eclipsed by, and separated from, presidential candidates in the election coverage of the two newspapers and three magazines for which data were collected. Of course, even presuming that these findings are representative of the pattern for the American print media as a whole, there is no direct evidence that such changes in election coverage have had any effect on attitudes in the electorate. The aggregate trends do match each other nicely, but left unanswered is the crucial question of whether people who are more exposed to a candidate-centered campaign in the media become less partisan as a result. The remainder of this chapter will examine the best available data on this relationship and the conditions that foster it.

The Data Base

Only uncontrolled media messages have been examined thus far. We will now turn to controlled media messages, for which data can be more easily linked to mass political attitudes. This inquiry will rely on information about seventy-eight campaigns for the House of Representatives in 1978. Data about media expenditures and other aspects of the campaign were gathered by Michael Traugott and Edie Goldenberg in their survey of Democratic and Republican congressional campaign managers.[8] Because the interviews with the campaign managers were conducted in the same districts as the 1978 CPS Election Study, it is possible to investigate whether the districts with heavy media campaigns are also those where the saliency of political parties in the electorate is lowest.

Such a cross-sectional correlation does not, however,

provide evidence from which to infer a definitive causal relationship. In fact, the causality probably operates to some degree in both directions, with reliance on the media weakening partisan attitudes in the electorate and with low levels of partisanship increasing the probability of waging a more candidate-centered media campaign. However, regardless of the causality underlying the relationship, its existence indicates that the media are playing a role in the process of transforming the public's focus on politics from parties to candidates.

The Decline of Partisanship in Congressional Elections

The use of congressional-year data represents a significant departure from the presidential orientation of the rest of this work. Thus a brief look at partisanship in congressional elections may be helpful at this point.

For many years it was a point of conventional wisdom that congressional elections are primarily partisan affairs in which voters cast their ballots for the candidate of their party, with little or no knowledge of the candidates.[9] To be sure, some deviations from the normal vote were to be expected, but by and large national forces, rather than individual candidates, were thought to be at the root of such deviations.[10] However, over the last several years many researchers have come to question whether such an interpretation of congressional elections remains valid. The percentage of party-line votes cast in congressional elections has fallen steadily from 84 percent in 1958 to only 69 percent in 1978. In fact, in 1976 more votes were actually cast according to party lines in the presidential race than for the House.[11] That parties are far less important to the electorate than in the past during congressional elections can be shown clearly by comparing the responses to the open-ended questions in the two congressional years for which such data are available. In 1958 only 23.7 percent of the electorate could be classified as neutral toward both parties, compared to 45.7 percent in 1978. Interestingly, the decline in salience from the presidential to congressional year is much steeper in the latter period, indicating that these attitudes are now less likely to endure to the off-year as well as being less stable from one presidential election to the next (see Chapter 2).

Unfortunately, like/dislike questions concerning congressional candidates were asked only in 1978, but it seems likely that if there were comparable data for 1958 the trend would show a greater degree of saliency. As Thomas Mann has written, "Increasingly, congressmen are responsible for their own margins of victory or defeat, and the electoral constraints they face are defined largely in their individual districts."[12] Through the media, congressional candidates now have the capability of making themselves far more visible than in the past, and to the degree that their campaigns are run independently of party one would expect a decline in the saliency and intensity of partisan attitudes in the electorate.

Media Expenditures and Partisan Attitudes

In order to test this hypothesis, we will employ two different measures for which comparable indices can be constructed concerning attitudes about both parties and candidates. The first involves simply counting the number of responses to the like/dislike questions in order to create interval level salience measures for purposes of correlational analysis. The second measure makes use of the intensity of respondents' feeling thermometer ratings precisely along the same lines of distance from the neutral point as described in Chapter 4.

For the purposes of this analysis, campaigns are best specified as interactive events in which voters can learn about specific candidates and parties from the efforts of both sides. For example, the salience of the Democratic Party may be just as much due to the negative advertising undertaken by the Republicans as the positive appeals by the Democrats. Therefore, the candidate and party salience and intensity measures are calculated on the basis of respondents' attitudes in each district toward both the Democrats and Republicans. Similarly, the major independent variable of this analysis, the amount of money spent on media advertising,[13] involves adding together what the two campaign managers estimated their campaign expenses to be in this area.

Table 6.1 shows the relationship between the amount of money spent in the campaign on media (both mass media and other media, such as billboards and buttons) and candidate and party salience and intensity. It is hardly sur-

Table 6.1 Correlations between advertising/media expenses and party and candidate salience and intensity measures

	Candidates	Parties	
Feeling thermometers[a]	.31	−.19	(n = 78)
Likes/dislikes[b]	.39	−.12	(n = 78)

a. This measure represents the average distance from 50 degrees which respondents in each district rate the candidates or parties.

b. This measure represents the mean number of likes and dislikes expressed by the respondents in each district.

SOURCE: 1978 CPS National Election Study and Traugott-Goldenberg Study of Campaign Managers.

prising to find that as the two candidates advertise more they become more salient to the general public—after all, that is part of the purpose of their doing so. However, it is not self-evident that a higher level of campaign media expenses should be associated with a lower degree of party salience in the electorate, as is shown by the two negative correlations in Table 6.1. If partisanship were stressed in campaigns, one might expect both sets of correlations to be positive. But apparently the effect of candidates' media advertising is solely the projection of candidate images, and not that of party images. Although the negative correlations between media expenses and partisanship are not of great magnitude, the cumulative effect of such a pattern over time could possibly account for a significant portion of the long-term trend.[14]

The Mediating Effect of Local Party Organizations

It should not be assumed, however, that media advertising has the same degree of effect on partisan attitudes under all conditions, for the media are used differently in some circumstances than in others. One of the factors that may affect the relationship between media advertising and partisanship is the strength of the local party organizations in the district. Although party machines capable of single-handedly electing candidates have virtually disappeared, party organizations nevertheless still play a significant role in determining the electoral outcome in many areas of the country. Of all the campaign managers who were interviewed in 1978, 12 percent said that they thought their party organization would be very important in determining the outcome of the general election for Congress in their district, 15 percent stated it was quite important, 30 percent fairly important, 29 percent not very important, and 14 percent stated that it was not at all important.[15]

Because the level of analysis for this portion of analysis is the congressional district, the responses from both managers in each race were combined in order to create a variable measuring the importance of local party organizations. In twenty-six districts both managers stated that the party organization would be at least fairly important in determining the electoral outcome; in thirty-five others, either both managers said their organization was not important or else one manager said it was only fairly important and the other said it was not important. (The seventeen cases where one manager said the organization was very or quite important and the opponent said it was not important have been excluded from this section of analysis.)

Table 6.2 demonstrates that when the party organizations are judged to be important in influencing the vote, the relationship between media expenses and candidate and party salience and intensity are quite different from when the organizations are not perceived as important. With both the feeling thermometers and the like/dislike measures, correlations between media expenditures and partisanship are much more negative in districts where the organizations are unimportant than where they are important. It may be that candidates simply do not have any reason to orient their media strategy toward any sort of partisan appeal when the organization is not important, for such tactics are not likely to be beneficial to them.

That party organizations do have the potential to be of substantial aid to candidates, however, is indirectly indicated by the much lower correlations between media ex-

Table 6.2 Correlations between salience and intensity measures and media expenses by strength of local party organizations

	Candidates	Parties	
Feeling thermometers			
Party organizations important	.18	−.09	(n = 26)
Party organizations not important	.50	−.42	(n = 35)
Like/dislikes			
Party organizations important	.26	−.02	(n = 26)
Party organizations not important	.64	−.21	(n = 35)

SOURCE: 1978 CPS National Election Study and Traugott-Goldenberg Study of Campaign Managers.

penditures and the candidate salience and intensity measures where the organizations are judged by the managers to be important. It is unlikely that money spent on the media in these districts is less effective. Rather, it is more plausible that where party organizations are strong, the amount of money spent on the media will have less effect on the projection of candidate images because it represents a much smaller proportion of the total communications from the candidates to the voters. In these areas, other activities—such as canvassing by the organizations—may be substantially responsible for levels of candidate salience, and this may reduce the correlations with the level of media advertising.

To summarize briefly, the strength of the local party organization is an important intervening variable in the relationship between media expenditures and the party and

candidate salience and intensity measures. Where the
parties are not thought by campaign managers to be important in determining the outcome, the degree of media
advertising is more negatively related to party salience
and intensity and more positively related to candidate salience and intensity.

Mass Media Versus Other Media

All media are not alike. Thus far, a variety of types of
media expenses—from TV ads to billboards—have been
lumped together to represent all the efforts of the candidates to put themselves in touch with the voters. Fortunately, the managers were also asked to estimate how
they allocated their advertising/media budgets. The most
important distinction that can be made between types of
media expenses is that between mass media (TV, radio,
and newspapers) and more indirect media (campaign literature, buttons, billboards, and so on). The latter are obviously more dependent on backing from a strong
organization, as such advertising requires someone to
pass out the literature and buttons and put up the yard
signs. In contrast, money can easily buy all the skills necessary to make mass media advertisements effective.

One would expect, therefore, that in districts where the
party organizations are important, a greater percentage of
campaign advertising will be devoted to media other than
TV, radio, or newspapers. While campaign strategies are
not always based entirely on rational considerations, it
would be surprising not to find that campaigns make more
use of these media when it is more feasible and pro-
ductive to do so. Indeed, it is found that in districts where
the local party organizations are not important candidates

allocate roughly 20 percent more of their budget to the mass media than in districts where the organizations are perceived to be strong—73 versus 54 percent.

The consequences of this difference are illustrated in Table 6.3. Evidently, mass media advertising is negatively related to partisanship regardless of whether or not the local party organizations are important—perhaps because the mass media orient advertising toward the projection of candidate images rather than party images. Even if a congressional candidate should go out of his or her way to attempt to portray a partisan image through the mass media, the crucial fact is that the voters are looking at, listening to, and reading about the candidates. The partisanship measures, however, show a different pattern in areas with strong organizations compared to those with weak organizations. Where the party organizations are not important, spending on both types of media is negatively related to party saliency and intensity, but in areas with strong party organizations only the correlation with mass media expenditures is negative. The reason for this difference probably has to do with the way these other types of media advertising are disseminated. It is easy to see how partisanship might suffer if autonomous candidate-centered organizations are completely responsible for distributing this material, but when party organizations participate in passing out leaflets and other material one should not expect to find such an effect.

One might even expect to find a strong positive correlation under the latter circumstance. However, American local party organizations are usually not very active and haven't been for decades. For example, Samuel Eldersveld found that in Detroit in 1956 that parties were far

Table 6.3 Correlations between salience and intensity measures and amount of mass and other media expenses by strength of local party organizations

	Candidates		Parties	
	Feeling thermometers	Likes/ dislikes	Feeling thermometers	Likes/ dislikes
Party organizations important				
Mass media	.09	.27	−.27	−.22
Other media	.00	−.06	.04	−.03
				(n = 26)
Party organizations not important				
Mass media	.46	.61	−.37	−.15
Other media	.29	.42	−.49	−.12
				(n = 35)

SOURCE: 1978 CPS National Election Study and Traugott-Goldenberg Study of Campaign Managers.

from "monolithic efficiency structures."[16] Less than one-fifth of the local organizations could be classified as operating near the peak of their potential performance on organizational tasks, according to Eldersveld. Similarly, Charles Clapp found that congressional participants in a 1958 Brookings roundtable discussion felt that party organizations were ineffective in providing support. As one Congressman stated, "If we depended on the party organization to get elected, none of us would be here."[17]

In sum, weak as they may be elsewhere, in districts where party organizations are considered to be unimportant by the campaign managers, media expenditures are much more negatively related to party salience and intensity for two reasons. First, where the organizations are most important, a smaller percentage of the candidate's media budget is allocated to the mass media, and the mass media are particularly conducive to projecting candidate rather than party images. Second, when party organizations are important, the amount of money spent on other types of media is not negatively correlated with party salience, for the organization participates at least to some degree in these activities.

However, the potential of local parties to reverse the decline of partisan attitudes in the electorate should not be exaggerated. Even if local parties were to become better organized and effective in the near future, there is little they could do to prevent the probable increase in direct candidate appeals through the mass media. Furthermore, it is likely that local parties will become even more dispensable to candidates as political action committees (PACs) continue to multiply and provide services that previously were often provided by the parties.

The Role of PAC Campaign Contributions

The post-Watergate campaign finance reforms have had a major effect on how political campaigns are run in the United States. One of the most notable changes involves the rapid growth of PACs, each of which represents a specific interest group rather than the aggregation of groups that a party represents. PAC contributions to congressional campaigns have grown steadily in recent years. In 1978 PAC contributions amounted to one-quarter of the funds raised by congressional candidates compared to only 7 percent for parties.[18] Some observers, such as Fred Wertheimer of Common Cause, have even speculated that soon PACs will virtually dominate congressional campaigns.

In the context of this chapter the growth of PACs is important for two reasons. First, PACs threaten to further displace the party organizations as a useful tool for political candidates. Not only are they contributing significant amounts of money to campaigns, they are also rapidly learning how to aid candidates in organizational tasks. Second, PAC money is interested money and therefore bound to have an influence on how campaigns are conducted. It is increasingly difficult for candidates to make broad partisan appeals when their campaign treasuries become dependent on pleasing a variety of special interests.

The first hypothesis stated above—that PACs threaten to further displace the party organizations—is clearly supported by the data. Dividing districts into roughly equal thirds according to the percentage of campaign expenditures contributed by PACs reveals that the likelihood of the manager responding that the party organization was important declines from 56, to 35, to 31 percent as PAC contributions increase. Because of the cross-sectional nature of the data, however, the causality of this relationship must remain somewhat uncertain. In part, it may be due to a rational calculation on the part of the PACs concerning where their money would most likely be influential. However, from a dynamic perspective it seems inevitable that as PAC contributions come to make up a larger percentage of campaign budgets, other factors such as local party organizations will become less important to the candidates.

In addition, as hypothesized above, PAC contributions are also likely to influence the nature of communication messages stressed by campaigns. Thus the proportion of money contributed by PACs should have an effect on the relationship between partisanship and campaign media expenditures. As demonstrated in Table 6.4, the level of media expenditures is far more negatively correlated with the partisanship measures in districts where PACs contributed most heavily than in those where PACS had least importance. Furthermore, this difference is independent of the strength of local party organizations, as indicated by the partial correlation coefficients.

The results presented in this chapter confirm the frequent assertion of media research that although media appeals may not be able to tell citizens what to think, they can profoundly influence what people think *about*. One of the most astute political cartoons concerning the media in recent years pictures a young boy asking his father, "Dad, if a tree falls in the forest, and the media aren't there to cover it, has the tree really fallen?"[19] Political parties do still exist despite their neglect by the media, but the gen-

Table 6.4 Correlations between advertising/media expenses and salience and intensity measures by percentage of expenditures contributed by PACs

	Candidates	Parties	
Feeling thermometers			
Low (0–16%)	.41 (.43)[a]	.02 (−.02)	(n = 19)[b]
Medium (17–33%)	.39 (.39)	.08 (−.14)	(n = 23)
High (over 33%)	.40 (.60)	−.35 (−.44)	(n = 17)
Likes/dislikes			
Low (0–16%)	.41 (.53)	−.12 (−.03)	(n = 19)
Medium (17–33%)	.34 (.44)	−.20 (−.30)	(n = 23)
High (over 33%)	.65 (.79)	−.25 (−.31)	(n = 17)

a. Correlations in parentheses represent partial correlations controlling for whether the party organizations in the district are judged to be important by the managers.

b. Case numbers are slightly less for the partial correlations because some districts cannot be categorized as having either strong or weak organizations.

SOURCE: 1978 CPS National Election Study and Traugott-Goldenberg Study of Campaign Managers.

eral emphasis of media campaigns on candidates rather than parties has served to make them less institutionally relevant and salient to the mass public.

The ultimate question to consider is whether such changes have been beneficial to the functioning of American democracy. One might argue that the shift in electoral salience should foster better representation as the electorate becomes more informed about congressional candidates. However, what voters know about the candidates on this level apparently has little to do with issues. Only 14 percent of the likes and dislikes expressed about the candidates for Congress in 1978 could be said to be references about matters of public policy, compared to 47 percent of the responses about political parties. As Miller and Stokes concluded in their classic study of constituency influence in Congress during the late 1950s, the party symbol performs a crucial linkage in the representation process because "the constituency can infer the candidates' position with more than random accuracy even though what the constituency has learned directly about these stands is almost nothing."[20] With parties becoming increasingly less likely to perform this linkage and without voter knowledge of congressional candidates' positions, the chances for faithful representation are clearly reduced.

7
Demographic Trends

The previous two chapters have documented the effects of the political factors of leadership and the media on the decline in the salience of party. Whenever a secular trend in political behavior is discovered, however, long-term demographic changes must always be considered as a possible cause. Over a period of several decades there will necessarily be a tremendous amount of population replacement, and new entrants into the electorate may be quite different from their elders demographically in such a way that their political attitudes differ as well. Under such a scenario, changes in the composition of the electorate, rather than changes among those already in the electorate, may be primarily responsible for the decline of partisanship. One could thus readily interpret the decline as something that should not have been unexpected, given the nature of recent demographic shifts. Therefore, if it can be shown that nonpolitical, demographic factors have *not* been responsible for the decline of partisanship, then the argument in favor of real-world changes in the conduct of American politics will be further strengthened.

Two basic changes in the composition of the electorate

stand out as the most plausible demographic factors for the decline of partisanship. First, the level of formal education has risen steadily in the electorate over the last several decades, and hence voters may now be better prepared to make political judgments without the aid of partisan cues. Second, there is the possibility that the decline may be limited to the influx of new voters into the electorate, whose generation has experienced a fundamentally different socialization process from that of previous generations. Both of these potential explanations will be examined in this chapter.

Education

As Philip Converse has remarked, the growth of higher education is probably the most massive social change to be found in the SRC/CPS election study time series.[1] In 1952 only 15 percent of the population had received some college education and the training of 41 percent was limited to no more than grade school. By 1980 the educational balance had flipped to the point where 37 percent had attended college while only 12 percent had just a grade school education.

The thesis that better-educated voters should have a weaker sense of partisanship can be found in numerous sources in the academic literature. For example, Everett Carll Ladd and Charles D. Hadley write that one main effect of the explosion of higher education "has been to expand dramatically the proportion of the population which feels no need for parties as active intermediaries in the voting decision."[2] Or as Frank Sorauf writes, party loyalty makes demands that the educated citizen is less willing to accommodate. These more educated voters are too well informed politically to "divide the political world into two simple categories, ours and theirs," according to Sorauf.[3] In sum, the theoretical basis for relating changes in education to the erosion of partisanship in the electorate depends quite heavily on a rationalistic view of the partisanship concept. According to this perspective, partisanship is primarily a device by which uninformed and uninvolved voters can avoid dealing with the complexities of the political world.

Despite the tremendous growth of higher education, however, there is little evidence that the electorate is much more involved in, or informed about, politics than in the 1950s. There has been an increase in several forms of political participation, such as letter writing to public officials, but these have been fairly slight in magnitude.[4] Furthermore, the most important form of participation— voting—has actually declined. As for the electorate's level of political sophistication, there has been a rise of about 14 percent in the proportion of the population that conceptualizes politics in abstract ideological terms,[5] but on specific issues people were no more likely to hold stable attitudes in the 1950s than in the 1970s.[6] And finally, on the most basic level, the public still remains strikingly uninformed about many political events and issues. For example, only 15 percent of those interviewed after the 1980 election could correctly identify which party had won the most seats in the House of Representatives and only 22 percent knew that Ronald Reagan advocated a 30 percent cut in federal income taxes.

Thus, on close examination, the hypothesized relationship between the growth of education and the decline of partisanship appears quite weak theoretically. If greater education has not produced a much more involved and informed electorate, then why should it have played any role in the weakening of partisanship? Indeed, Figures 7.1–7.4 demonstrate that the decline of partisanship has been nearly identical across all educational levels.

First, on strength of party identification we see that

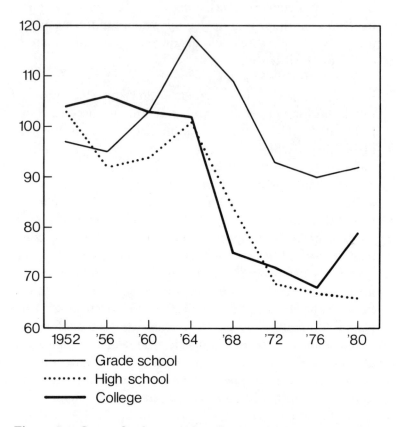

Figure 7.1 Strength of party identification by level of education, 1952–1980

Note: See Table 4.3 for a description of the strength of party identification index used in this figure.

Source: SRC/CPS National Election Studies.

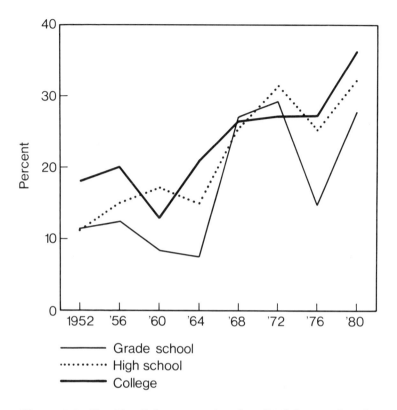

Figure 7.2   Presidential-congressional split-ticket voting by level of education, 1952–1980
Source: SRC/CPS National Election Studies.

higher education has not always been synonymous with the greatest sense of independence (see Figure 7.1). In fact, from 1952 to 1960 college-educated citizens actually displayed the highest level of party identification, and only in 1968 were they lowest on the index. It is true that since 1964 grade school-educated respondents have consistently been the most strongly partisan, but this is

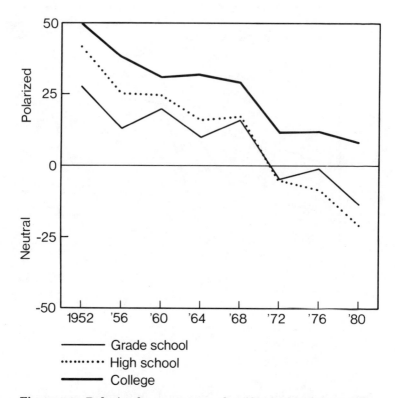

Figure 7.3   Polarized versus neutral evaluations of the parties by level of education, 1952–1980

Note: Figure entries represent the proportion of respondents positive toward one party and negative toward the other on the like/dislike questions minus the proportion neutral toward both parties.

Source: SRC/CPS National Election Studies.

largely a spurious relationship because older people have come to be greatly overrepresented among those with only a grade school education.[7] What is important about Figure 7.1 is that it shows that the decline in strength of party identification has been roughly parallel from one education bracket to another. Similarly, from the data displayed in Figure 7.2 we can draw much the same conclusions regarding split-ticket voting. The static relationship between education and splitting one's ticket has varied considerably over the years, indicating that such behavior is by no means restricted only to better educated voters, and dynamically the increase is roughly equal in each of the three categories of educational training.

Figures 7.3 and 7.4, which display data from the like/dislike and feeling thermometer questions discussed in Chapter 6, also show similar patterns of decline across

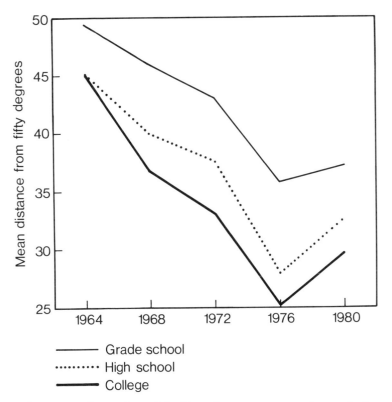

Figure 7.4 Intensity of feeling thermometer ratings of the parties by level of education, 1964–1980
Source: SRC/CPS National Election Studies.

educational groups. In both cases, however, one can also discern a consistent difference by education in attitudes toward the parties that sheds some light on the nature of the difference between the two measures. On the like/dislike probes the responses of those who have had some college education are always the most skewed toward polarized rather than neutral views of the parties (see Figure 7.3). This is quite likely due to the greater ability to articulate one's feelings that comes with a higher education. College-educated citizens are less likely to be classified as neutral simply as a result of an inability to respond to the open-ended questions. A higher education also contributes to a more moderate view of the world in which extreme attitudes become tempered.[8] Thus, when we turn to the intensity of respondents' feeling thermometer ratings of the parties, the relationship between partisan attitudes and education is found to be just the reverse of the pattern of the like/dislike data, with the college-educated being the least intensely partisan (see Figure 7.4).

These two opposing relationships between partisan attitudes and education provide further theoretical evidence that the growth of education cannot be responsible for the decline of partisanship. Holding everything else constant, the growth of education should have resulted in contradictory rather than similar patterns over time. However, as with strength of party identification and split-ticket voting, there have evidently been factors causing a decline in partisanship equally among all education groups.

Generational Replacement

One such possible factor is another demographic trend—generational replacement. Indeed, generational differences have been perhaps the most widely discussed and thoroughly investigated reason for the decline of parties in the electorate. Thus, given that we can rely heavily on other sources, our empirical treatment of this subject need not be as detailed as with education.

The evidence clearly shows that the decline in strength of party identification has come more from new entrants to the political system than from those who have abandoned already established ties. Arthur Miller and Warren Miller outline three age-related factors that have contributed to the decline of party identification. First, young nonpartisans have replaced older partisans; second, each new entering cohort has been less partisan; and finally, although there has been less change among those already in the electorate than among new voters, the former group has also declined somewhat in party strength.[9]

Left unanswered in this discussion is the key question of what has caused new entrants into the electorate to be so much weaker in party identification than their parents were at the same age. Paul Allen Beck's socialization theory of realignment provides an intriguing possible explanation.[10] Beck argues that the periodicity with which realignments have occurred throughout U.S. history has been a function of cyclical changes in the partisan socialization process. According to this theory, after a realignment occurs parents will be very conscious of the issues on which the new alignment has turned and will strongly transmit their partisan attachments to their offspring. These children of realignment, however, will be less successful in passing their party identification on to the next generation, because by this time the realigning issues will have faded as matters of serious political concern. As a result, the entrance of this less partisan generation into the electorate will contribute to a process of dealignment.

In addition, as a large, unmobilized block of voters, this generation also represents the potential for the next realignment on the basis of new issues.

Given that the last realignment occurred in the mid-1930s, Beck's theory nicely predicts the timing and generational nature of the decline in strength of party identification. It does not, however, fit quite so well with the more secular aspects of the decline of parties in the electorate. For example, although party identification has not eroded substantially among older cohorts, these voters have nevertheless followed the general trend toward split-ticket voting. As Nie et al. conclude, "The rise of split ticket voting appears to be more a function of the pressures of the period than the generation of the voter."[11]

If the partisan behavior patterns of older and younger voters have followed the same tendencies, then the fact that older voters have retained their partisan labels may be of little political significance—the identification may still be present but it may well mean much less to these citizens than in the past. Turning to the data from the like/dislike questions and feeling thermometers, it is clear that such is in fact the case. Figure 7.5 shows that all cohorts have moved toward a neutral evaluation of the parties, and Figure 7.6 shows that each has come to rate the parties with far less intensity on the feeling thermometers. Thus it is apparent that the generational nature of the decline in strength of party identification has been the exception rather than the rule. Older generations may have largely held on to their partisan labels, which were acquired during a period when the parties were more meaningful to voters than they are now, but the labels no longer have the importance they once had for these cohorts.

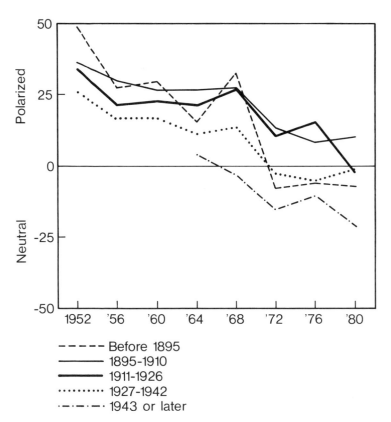

Figure 7.5 Polarized versus neutral evaluations of the parties by age cohorts, 1952–1980
Note: See Figure 7.3 for a description of the index used in this figure.
Source: SRC/CPS National Election Studies.

The findings presented in this chapter have demonstrated that neither education nor generational replacement has played a major role in the decline of political partisanship. These negative results make it evident that long-term factors involving changes in the character of

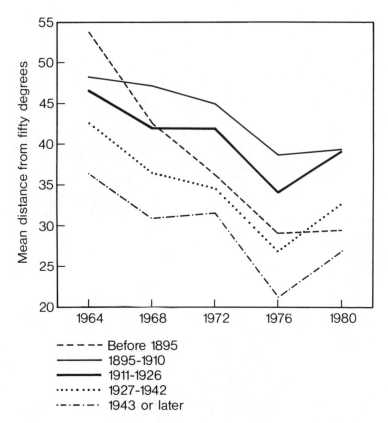

Figure 7.6 Intensity of feeling thermometer ratings of the parties by age cohorts, 1964–1980
Source: SRC/CPS National Election Studies.

American politics have caused people of all ages and all education brackets to change in their attitudes toward the parties. The political explanations for the decline of partisanship fit the data far better than the sociological explanations examined in this chapter.

8
The Public as an Echo Chamber

In his last book, *The Responsible Electorate,* V. O. Key outlined a basic theory of political behavior that came frequently to mind as I wrote this book. According to Key, "The voice of the people is but an echo chamber. The output of an echo chamber bears an inevitable and invariable relation to the input. As candidates and parties clamor for attention and vie for popular support, the people's verdict can be no more than a selective reflection from among the alternatives and outlooks presented to them."[1] The explanation for party decline in the electorate that has been argued in this book squares nicely with Key's echo chamber analogy.

The public did not decide all of a sudden that parties were bankrupt political institutions and mandate their decline. Rather, voters reacted gradually over the last quarter of a century to the way in which politics was presented to them. Political parties themselves became less institutionally relevant and the public adjusted their views of them accordingly. As party leaders have come to act more and more on their own initiative and to communicate with voters directly through the media, the public has increasingly come to see the crucial short-term domestic and foreign issues only in terms of the candidates. It is candidates rather than parties that are now viewed as being responsible for solving, or failing to solve, our current political problems. Therefore, the parties are receiving much less credit or blame for political outcomes than they did several decades ago. Despite the decay in public confidence in American political institutions in recent years, people have not turned sharply negative toward the parties. Instead they have come to see political parties as less relevant to what goes on in the everyday world of politics, and hence have become far more neutral toward them.

If the answer to the phenomenon of party decline in the electorate can in fact be found in the real world of elite political maneuvering, one might question why it is necessary to analyze mass survey data. My reply would be that although public opinion acts something like an echo chamber, without survey data one can never be sure just *what* people are reacting to. After all, there have been major political catastrophies (Vietnam, Watergate, economic recessions) for both parties in recent years, which could quite reasonably have led many voters to become negative toward both. Yet the change in the public's attitudes about the parties has been shaped not so much by specific political events as by how the events have been handled by leaders and presented by the media.

In order to reinvigorate political partisanship in the future, then, the public must be convinced that political parties perform a useful function in the American political process. The challenge that the parties face is not merely to espouse programs with popular appeal, but also to demonstrate that they play a crucial political role—

from the recruitment of leaders to the implementation of policies. If the echo chamber analogy is correct, then it is reasonable to assume that if leaders begin once again to act as partisans and be presented by the media as such, the decline of partisanship in the electorate can potentially be reversed.

The need for such a revitalization is hardly a new theme. Over thirty years ago a committee of distinguished political scientists concluded that our party system was functioning poorly in sustaining well-considered programs and mobilizing public support for them.[2] Numerous recommendations were compiled, all of which the scholars believed would facilitate a more responsible and effective party system—one that would be accountable to the public and able to deal with the problems of modern government.

These suggestions became an instant source of controversy and were justifiably criticized for their unrealistic call for more disciplined, programmatic, and ideologically distinctive parties in a political culture in which interests are too diverse to be expressed in the centralized fashion outlined in the recommendations.[3] Despite this critical flaw, however, what remains the central problem of the American party system was illuminated—namely, the relevance of political parties in solving governmental problems: "The party in power has a responsibility, broadly defined, for the general management of the government, for its manner of getting results achieved, for the consequences of inaction as well as action, for the intended and unintended outcome of its conduct of public affairs, for all that it plans to do, for all that it might have foreseen, for the leadership it provides, for the acts of all its agents, and for what it says as well as for what it does."[4] The sense of these scholars in 1950 that the parties were not adequately meeting their responsibilities led them to send out an alarm that a serious problem existed; the fact that parties are now even less capable of meeting these responsibilities is reflected in the survey data results presented in this book.

The skeptic might examine the long history of concern with the future of American political parties and conclude that some have cried wolf at least once too often. After all, over three decades later the two parties still remain intact in the world's oldest surviving party system. There seems to be no danger that the parties will suddenly vanish from the scene and leave catastrophic political and social chaos in their wake. The "party" is far from over, as Samuel Eldersveld has recently concluded.[5]

But although parties have not disintegrated they have clearly declined in relevance, and the consequences have been significant. In 1950 the scholars foresaw several dangers if no action was taken to make the party system more responsible. Their warnings seem eerily prophetic over three decades later; their fears have turned into our present-day realities. Indeed, examining what they saw as the dangers of a weakened party system illuminates some of our current problems.

A major fear was that if the parties could not develop comprehensive programs that could be successfully implemented, voter frustration might set in motion more extreme tendencies of both the left and the right, leading to a deep political cleavage "to which neither our political institutions nor our civic habits are adapted."[6] This fear has been at least partially realized in the turmoil of the 1960s and the development of strident single-issue groups. Parties once channeled political conflict and kept policy differences within reasonable bounds. One result of the decline of partisanship is that we now have a system that is capable of expressing a wide diversity of viewpoints but is rather poor at aggregating them. With parties increasingly less able to resolve these conflicts, the tone of American politics is becoming more negative and bitter, and policy compromises are much harder to come by.

A second possible consequence mentioned was the danger of overextending the presidency. As the only branch of government capable of leadership direction and unity of action, the presidency is the logical institution to expect the unmet responsibilities of the parties to fall upon. The problem with placing such expectations on the President is that "either his party becomes a flock of sheep or the party falls apart. In effect this concept of the presidency disposes of the party system by making the President reach directly for the support of a majority of votes. It favors a President who exploits skillfully the arts of demagoguery, who uses the whole country as his political backyard, and who does not mind turning into the embodiment of personal government."[7]

A generation before them, these political scientists speculated, such a prospect would have been dismissed as "fantastic." Today it is part of the modern presidency. Major policy proposals are presented to the public first and foremost as *presidential* programs. The economic program of the current administration, for example, is widely referred to not as Republican economics but as "Reaganomics." Of course it is members of the press rather than the president who have pinned this label on the program. However, as shown in Chapter 6, such press concentration on the president and presidential candidates has increasingly become the norm. It is no wonder that within such a political context the American public has become increasingly indifferent to the parties.

In 1950 just such a prospect was foreseen if party accountability were not restored. That the public might "turn its back upon the two parties" was a real possibility, and was in fact already beginning to occur: "Present conditions are a great incentive for the voters to dispose of the parties as intermediaries between themselves and the government. In a way, a sizeable body of the electorate has shifted from hopeful interest in the parties to the opposite attitude. This mass of voters sees itself as the President's or his opponent's direct electoral support."[8] Over three decades later this statement is now even more true.

Partisanship once provided the American electorate with a sense of continuity and stability. With its decline many citizens have been set adrift without an anchor in a political world full of strong eddies and currents. As a result, some no longer vote;[9] others are swept first one way and then another by the currents, causing the much talked-about rise of political volatility. Throughout the 1980 campaign political commentators frequently remarked on the high degree of changeability in voter preferences. One pointed indication of this volatility is the large percentage of voters who waited until very near the end of the campaign before they decided how to vote. In *The American Voter,* Campbell and his colleagues noted that most voters in 1952 and 1956 had made up their minds by the time of the nominating conventions, indicating "that the psychological forces guiding behavior arise before the campaign opens."[10] In 1980, however, half of the voters interviewed stated that they had made their decisions during the campaign, and an unprecedented 9 percent waited *until election day* to make up their minds (only 2 percent did so in each of the Eisenhower-Stevenson contests).

What was most striking about the last-minute decision-making in the 1980 campaign was the suddenness with which a virtually even race turned into a landslide victory for Ronald Reagan. As might be expected, given their lack of partisan direction, those who were neutral toward both parties on the like/dislike questions accounted for a large proportion (47.8 percent) of the undecided voters in the CPS preelection survey. Furthermore, they, much more than any other group of undecided voters, were swayed toward Reagan—casting an astounding 70.3 percent of their votes for him compared to 18.9 percent for Carter and 11.8 percent for Anderson. This is not to say that these voters alone accounted for the last-minute shift, but clearly it does indicate their great potential for volatile political behavior.

In conclusion, party coalitions in the United States have undergone a series of processes of decay over the last three decades, increasing the possibilities of *both* short-term and long-term change in the near future. With the weakening of the public's images of the parties, it is no wonder that volatility has become the new catchword of American politics. As the long-term forces that serve to anchor electoral behavior decline, the potential increases for large oscillations in the vote because of short-term issue and candidate factors. Furthermore, given that there is less of what V. O. Key called a "standing decision" for people to return to, there is also an increased potential for the translation of short-term forces into long-term ones. Such a process, however, will require that the issues and candidates responsible for the short-term changes become firmly linked with public images of the parties. When and if that happens, a new era of American electoral politics will have begun.

Notes

Introduction

1. E. E. Schattschneider, *Party Government* (New York: Farrar and Rinehart, 1942), p. 1.
2. David S. Broder, *The Party's Over: The Failure of Politics in America* (New York: Harper and Row, 1971), p. xxiii.
3. Morris P. Fiorina, "The Decline of Collective Responsibility in American Politics," *Daedalus* 109 (1980): 44.
4. Malcolm E. Jewell and David M. Olson, *American State Political Parties and Elections*, rev. ed. (Homewood, Ill.: Dorsey, 1982).
5. Cornelius Cotter and John F. Bibby, "Institutional Development of Parties and the Thesis of Party Decline," *Political Science Quarterly* 95 (1980): 1–27.
6. Austin Ranney, "The Political Parties: Reform and Decline," in Anthony King, ed., *The New American Political System* (Washington, D.C.: American Enterprise Institute, 1978), p. 215.
7. S. E. Finer, *The Changing British Party System, 1945–1979* (Washington, D.C.: American Enterprise Institute, 1980), p. xii.

1. The Concept of Political Partisanship

1. Jack Dennis, "Some Properties of Measures of Partisanship" (paper presented at the annual meeting of the American Political Science Association, 1981), p. 4.

2. See Paul Lazarfeld, Bernard Berelson, and Hazel Gaudet, *The People's Choice* (New York: Columbia University Press, 1944); and Bernard Berelson, Paul Lazarfeld, and William McPhee, *Voting: A Study of Opinion Formation in a Presidential Campaign* (Chicago: University of Chicago Press, 1954).

3. See Ian Budge, Ivor Crewe, and Dennis Fairlie, eds., *Party Identification and Beyond* (New York: Wiley, 1975).

4. See Philip E. Converse, "The Concept of a Normal Vote," in Angus Campbell et al., *Elections and the Political Order* (New York: Wiley, 1966); and Arthur H. Miller, "Normal Vote Analysis: Sensitivity to Change over Time," *American Journal of Political Science* 23, (1979): 406–423.

5. Party affiliation here has been defined as loosely as possible by including Independent leaners with the identifiers of each party. If one excludes these leaners, then only 2 percent of the 1972–1976 voters can be said to have shifted their identification from one party to the other between the two presidential elections.

6. Philip E. Converse and Georges Dupeux, "Politicalization of the Electorate in France and the United States," in Campbell et al., *Elections and the Political Order.*

7. Angus Campbell, Gerald Gurin, and Warren E. Miller, *The Voter Decides* (Evanston, Ill.: Row, Peterson and Co., 1954), p. 90.

8. Angus Campbell, Philip E. Converse, Warren E. Miller, and Donald E. Stokes, *The American Voter* (New York: Wiley 1960), p. 121.

9. Warren E. Miller, "The Cross-National Use of Party Identification as a Stimulus to Political Inquiry," in Budge, Crewe, and Fairlie, eds., *Party Identification and Beyond,* p. 22.

10. See Richard A. Brody and Benjamin I. Page, "Comment:

The Assessment of Policy Voting," *American Political Science Review* 66 (1972): 450–458; and Gregory B. Markus and Philip E. Converse, "A Dynamic Simultaneous Model of Electoral Choice," *American Political Science Review* 73 (1979): 406–423.

11. See Richard W. Boyd, "Decline of U.S. Voter Turnout: Structural Explanations," *American Politics Quarterly* 9 (1981): 133–159.

12. Anthony Downs, *An Economic Theory of Democracy* (New York: Harper and Row, 1957), p. 233.

13. Warren E. Miller and Donald E. Stokes, "Constituency Influence in Congress," in Campbell et al., *Elections and the Political Order.*

14. Morris P. Fiorina, *Retrospective Voting in American National Elections* (New Haven, Conn.: Yale University Press, 1981), pp. 89–90.

15. See Richard A. Brody, "Stability and Change in Party Identification: Presidential to Off-Years" (paper presented at the annual meeting of the American Political Science Association, 1977); and Gregory B. Markus, "The Political Environment and the Dynamics of Public Attitudes: A Panel Study," *American Journal of Political Science* 23 (1979): 338–359.

16. Charles H. Franklin and John E. Jackson, "The Dynamics of Party Identification" (paper presented at the annual meeting of the American Political Science Association, 1981), p. 18.

17. Herbert F. Weisberg, "A Multidimensional Conceptualization of Party Identification," *Political Behavior* 2 (1980): 33–60.

18. Jack Dennis, "Trends in Public Support for the American Party System," *British Journal of Political Science* 5 (1975): 230.

19. See Richard Hofstadter, *The Idea of a Party System* (Berkeley: University of California Press, 1969); and Austin Ranney, *Curing the Mischiefs of Faction: Party Reform in America* (Berkeley: University of California Press, 1975), chapter 2.

20. Walter Dean Burnham, *Critical Elections and the Mainsprings of American Politics* (New York: Norton, 1970).

21. One other possible problem concerns the decline of regionalism in party identification. When the distribution of partisanship in a district approaches an even split between Democrats and Republicans, as it has throughout the South and elsewhere, the level of ticket-splitting necessary to cause a split outcome declines. In other words, the same degree of individual-level ticket-splitting could theoretically be responsible for a substantially higher number of split outcomes.

22. Warren E. Miller and Teresa E. Levitan, *Leadership and Change: The New Politics and the American Electorate* (Cambridge, Mass.: Winthrop, 1976).

23. Patrick H. Caddell, "The Democratic Strategy and Its Electoral Consequences," in Seymour Martin Lipset, ed., *Party Coalitions in the 1980s* (San Francisco: Institute for Contemporary Studies, 1981), p. 300.

24. Dennis, "Trends in Public Support."

25. Converse, "The Concept of a Normal Vote."

26. Philip E. Converse, *The Dynamics of Party Support: Cohort-Analyzing Party Identification* (Beverly Hills, Calif.: Sage Publications, 1976).

27. Burnham, *Critical Elections,* pp. 130–131.

28. Gerald Pomper, "Impacts on the Political System," in Samuel Kirkpatrick, ed., *American Electoral Behavior: Change and Stability* (Beverly Hills, Calif.: Sage Publications, 1976), p. 137.

29. See Converse, *The Dynamics of Party Support,* pp. 106–111, for a lively discussion of these shocks.

30. Bruce Keith et al., "The Myth of the Independent Voter" (paper presented at the annual meeting of the American Political Science Association, 1977).

31. For the figures for each year individually see Warren E. Miller, "Policy Directions and Presidential Leadership: Alternative Interpretations of the 1980 Presidential Election" (paper presented at the annual meeting of the American Political Science Association, 1981).

32. Keith et al., "The Myth of the Independent Voter," p. 3.

33. Philip E. Converse and Gregory B. Markus, "Plus ça change . . . : The New CPS Election Study Panel," *American Political Science Review* 73 (1979): 32–49.

34. Philip E. Converse, "The Nature of Belief Systems in Mass Publics," in David E. Apter, ed., *Ideology and Discontent* (Glencoe, Ill.: Free Press, 1964).

35. Converse and Markus, "Plus ça change," p. 45.

36. See John A. Ferejohn, "On the Decline of Competition in Congressional Elections," *American Political Science Review* 71 (1977): 166–176; and Norman H. Nie, Sidney Verba, and John R. Petrocik, *The Changing American Voter* (Cambridge, Mass.: Harvard University Press, 1976).

2. The Stability of Partisan Attitudes

1. See David C. Valentine and John R. Van Wingen, "Partisanship, Independence, and the Partisan Identification Question," *American Politics Quarterly* 8 (1980): 165–186; Weisberg, "A Multidimensional Conceptualization of Party Identification"; and Dennis, "Some Properties of Measures of Partisanship."

2. Samuel J. Eldersveld, "The Independent Vote: Measurement, Characteristics and Implications for Party Strategy," *American Political Science Review* 46 (1952): 752.

3. Campbell et al., *The American Voter*, p. 144.

4. Christopher H. Achen, "Mass Political Attitudes and the Survey Response," *American Political Science Review* 69 (1975): 1218–31.

5. Since only three responses were coded to each question in the 1972 wave of the '72–'76 panel the indices in both panels have been constructed on the basis of the first three responses. The range of each index is thus from +3 to −3.

3. Independent or No Preference?

1. See Paul A. Abramson, "Generational Change and the Decline of Party Identification in America: 1952–1974," *Ameri-*

can Political Science Review 70 (1976): 469-478; and Converse, *The Dynamics of Party Support.*

2. See Campbell et al., *The American Voter;* Burnham, *Critical Elections;* Gerald Pomper, *Voter's Choice: Varieties of American Electoral Behavior* (New York: Dodd, Mead, 1975); and Herbert B. Asher, *Presidential Elections and American Politics,* 2d edition (Homewood, Ill.: Dorsey, 1980).

3. See John R. Petrocik, "An Analysis of the Intransitivities of Party Identification," *Political Methodology* 1 (1974): 31-47; Brody, "Stability and Change"; Keith et al., "The Myth of the Independent Voter"; and W. Philips Shively, "Information Costs and the Partisan Life Cycle" (paper presented at the annual meeting of the American Political Science Association, 1977).

4. Converse, *The Dynamics of Party Support,* p. 127.

5. In 1980 this procedure was standardized and documented for the first time. As stated in the codebook for the study, respondents were coded as apoliticals only if they showed little or no interest in response to questions regarding their interest in the campaign, concern about which party would win, intention to vote, and general attention to politics.

6. Since 1968 the responses to each of the questions in the party identification series have been coded separately in each dataset. Therefore, one can easily identify those people who initially say that they have "no preference" on the basis of the coded responses to the lead question. However, before 1968 only the traditional derived scale was coded. Thus I returned to the original interview protocols to obtain this information for 1964.

7. The analysis in this chapter begins with 1964 because it marks the last election year in Converse's steady-state period of strength of partisanship. Earlier years would therefore look much the same in all probability.

8. This change was not an artifact of lowering the voting age to eighteen in 1972, as the shift is virtually the same when those aged eighteen to twenty are excluded.

9. Because of the small number of cases in some years for

some of the categories, pooling the data from these five studies provides far more reliable estimates. There are of course some fluctuations from year to year, but the basic patterns are found consistently in each study.

10. In order to increase the sample size for these figures I have combined data from the P1, C1, and C3 waves of the 1980 study.

11. One plausible explanation for these patterns may be that as those with no preference are less politically involved than Independents, they will be more likely to agree with any statement in an interview situation. However, when other agree-disagree items are examined such a hypothesis is not confirmed.

4. Negativity or Neutrality?

1. Nie, Verba, and Petrocik, *The Changing American Voter*, pp. 57–58.

2. Kristi Andersen, "Generation, Partisan Shift, and Realignment: A Glance Back to the New Deal," in Nie, Verba, and Petrocik, *The Changing American Voter*, p. 95.

3. James L. Sundquist, *Dynamics of the Party System: Alignment and Realignment of Political Parties in the United States* (Washington, D.C.: The Brookings Institution, 1973), p. 353.

4. Nie, Verba, and Petrocik, *The Changing American Voter*, p. 283.

5. The wording of this question has changed slightly over the years. Listed below are the different versions that have been asked:

1952: "Do you think there are any important differences between what the Democratic and Republican parties stand for, or do you think they are about the same?"

1960, 1964, 1972–1980: "Do you think there are any important differences in what the Republicans and Democrats stand for?"

1968: "Do you think there are any important differences between the Republican and Democratic parties?"

6. This question has also undergone slight changes in wording over the years. In 1960, 1964 and 1968 respondents were asked which party they thought would be the most likely to do what they wanted on whichever problem they mentioned. In 1972 this was changed to asking which party would be the most likely to get the government to be helpful on the problem, and in 1976–1980 the wording was again changed to which party would be the most likely to do a better job in dealing with the problem.

7. Merle Black and George B. Rabinowitz, "American Electoral Change: 1952–1972 (with a note on 1976)," in William Crotty, ed., *The Party Symbol: Readings on Political Parties* (San Francisco: W. H. Freeman, 1980), p. 241.

8. I wish to thank M. Kent Jennings for making these data available to me, as well as for offering advice concerning their use.

9. See Abramson, "Generational Change."

10. Sundquist, *Dynamics of the Party System,* p. 343.

11. In 1972 CPS originally coded only the first three responses. The fourth and fifth responses were later coded by Arthur H. Miller. I wish to thank Professor Miller for making these data available to me.

12. Several technical differences between the like/dislike data that I have used and those that Nie et al. use should be noted. First, Nie et al. use only the first three responses in all years while I employ all five. Second, they fail to filter out the 100 respondents in 1952 and the 17 in 1960 who were not interviewed in the preelection wave. As these respondents were not asked the like/dislike questions they should be excluded from the analysis. Finally, Nie et al. include responses from the Black supplements in 1964 and 1968. Subsequent analysis at CPS has shown that these supplements actually introduce a greater degree of bias into the sample. Hence I have not used them.

13. The proportion without any positive or negative com-

ments for each year are as follows: 1952, 9.7%; 1956, 12.9%; 1960, 15.7%; 1964, 17.1%; 1968, 14.0%; 1972, 27.0%; 1976, 28.7%; 1980, 34.3%. The tiny remainder of those who fall under the neutral-neutral category in Table 4.4 express both likes and dislikes, with each like being matched by a dislike of the same party.

14. In the 1964 and 1968 studies those who responded "don't know" were coded at the 50 degree mark. Therefore, I have followed the same coding rule with the 1972–1980 data to ensure consistency throughout the time series.

15. Furthermore, there are two reasons to expect that this jump may be a methodological artifact of changes in the structure of the interview schedule in 1980. First, respondents were also asked to rate the "Democratic Party" and the "Republican Party" in the preelection interview. And second, the preelection interview in 1980 focused more on political parties than any other in the past. Both of these factors could well have caused respondents to think more about the parties than they would have otherwise and therefore rate them less neutrally. The reason such an effect is not found in the like/dislike questions is that these remained very early in the preelection interview whereas the 1980 feeling thermometer ratings shown in Table 4.5 are from the postelection wave.

16. Similarly, when asked which party would do a better job in handling inflation, only 42 percent of those interviewed in 1980 thought one party would do a better job than the other, and regarding unemployment the comparable figure was just 39 percent.

5. Political Leadership and the Parties

1. Campbell et al., *The American Voter*, p. 318.

2. Lester G. Seligman, "The Presidential Office and the President as Party Leader (with a Postscript on the Kennedy-Nixon Era)," in Jeff Fishel, ed., *Parties and Elections in an Anti-Party Age* (Bloomington: Indiana University Press, 1978), p. 300.

3. Schattschneider, *Party Government*, p. 64.

4. Donald M. Fraser, "Democratizing the Democratic Party," in Robert A. Goldwin, ed., *Political Parties in the Eighties* (Washington, D.C.: American Enterprise Institute), p. 129.

5. See Ranney, *Curing the Mischiefs of Faction;* William Crotty, *Political Reform and the American Experiment* (New York: Crowell, 1977); and Jeane J. Kirkpatrick, *Dismantling the Parties: Reflections on Party Reform and Party Decomposition* (Washington, D.C.: American Enterprise Institute, 1978).

6. See William R. Keech and Donald R. Matthews, *The Party's Choice* (Washington, D.C.: The Brookings Institution, 1976).

7. Barbara G. Farah, "Convention Delegates: Party Reform and the Representatives of Party Elites, 1972–1980" (paper presented at the annual meeting of the American Political Science Association, 1981).

8. See Thomas E. Patterson, *The Mass Media Election: How Americans Choose Their President* (New York: Praeger, 1980).

9. Ranney, "The Political Parties," p. 239.

10. Thomas E. Cronin, *The State of the Presidency,* 2d ed. (Boston: Little, Brown and Co., 1980), p. 246.

11. Hugh Heclo, "The Changing Presidential Office," in Arnold J. Meltsner, ed., *Politics and the Oval Office* (San Francisco: Institute for Contemporary Studies, 1981), pp. 168–169.

12. Morris P. Fiorina, *Congress: Keystone of the Washington Establishment* (New Haven, Conn.: Yale University Press, 1977).

13. See Nie, Verba, and Petrocik, *The Changing American Voter,* pp. 55–57.

14. The candidate evaluation data were originally gathered as part of a research project undertaken by Arthur H. Miller, who kindly granted me permission to use them. The dimensions of the party like/dislike questions have been constructed precisely according to the subheadings in the election study codebooks. The same is true for the candidate dimensions with the exception of that of general philosophy. Most of the

codes in this dimension can be found between 805 and 828 in the 1972 and 1976 codebooks. The distinction between responses on this dimension and those on domestic and foreign policy is that the former deals only with broad comments such as liberal, conservative, humanistic, anti-states' rights, pro-big government, and so on.

15. Quoted in Broder, *The Party's Over*, p. 6.

16. See Arthur H. Miller and Martin P. Wattenberg, "Policy and Performance Voting in the 1980 Election" (paper presented at the annual meeting of the American Political Science Association, 1981).

6. The Role of the Media

1. Robert Agranoff, *The Management of Electoral Campaigns* (Boston: Holbrook Press, 1976).

2. Fiorina, "The Decline of Collective Responsibility," p. 33.

3. Frank J. Sorauf, *Party Politics in America,* 4th ed. (Boston: Little, Brown and Co., 1980), p. 255.

4. Sundquist, *Dynamics of the Party System,* p. 351.

5. I am most grateful to the following undergraduates at the University of Michigan who collected these data: Carolyn Bradley, Debra Den Houter, Sally Everhard, Francis Gilbert, John Heidt, John Huget, Joseph Parke, Frank Raiford, Mark Tompkins, Nathaniel Warshay, and Becky Weinreich.

6. As each of the magazines contained so much less material because of its weekly rather than daily format, I have combined data from all three in order to have a large enough sample of articles to work with.

7. In part, this trend may be attributable to the decline in the sheer number of campaign-related stories per year. However, all coders were agreed that the length of the average story increased over time as the print medium struggled to compete with television by presenting the sort of in-depth coverage that television is generally not capable of. It is therefore

difficult to judge, without going through the arduous task of counting column inches, whether the amount of election coverage in fact decreased substantially. The sense of the coders was that there was somewhat less material to code over time, but certainly not to the degree necessary to account for the trend displayed in Figure 6.3.

8. I wish to thank Michael Traugott and Edie Goldenberg for kindly making these data available to me.

9. Donald E. Stokes and Warren E. Miller, "Party Government and the Saliency of Congress," *Public Opinion Quarterly* 26 (1962): 531–546.

10. See, for example, Edward R. Tufte, "Determinants of the Outcome of Midterm Congressional Elections," *American Political Science Review* 69 (1975): 812–826.

11. Thomas E. Mann and Raymond E. Wolfinger, "Candidates and Parties in Congressional Elections," *American Political Science Review* 74 (1980): 617–632.

12. Thomas E. Mann, *Unsafe at Any Margin* (Washington, D.C.: American Enterprise Institute, 1978), p. 3.

13. This measure is derived from the managers' estimates of the proportion of their total campaign budget allocated to "advertising/media."

14. Although these correlations have been calculated on the basis of data about only seventy-eight congressional districts, it should be kept in mind that the mass-level data from each district consists of approximately twenty interviews for a total of roughly sixteen hundred. One could thus match the campaign managers' data to each respondent in the appropriate district and then perform the same correlations on a sample size twenty times greater. However, the theoretical focus of this chapter is to explain variance between districts rather than variance within districts. Therefore, in order to eliminate variance within districts, mean scores have been used throughout this analysis.

15. In all but a few cases where no preelection interview was obtained, this question was asked before the election. Therefore, the responses are not subject to rationalization based on the outcome of the election.

16. Samuel J. Eldersveld, *Political Parties: A Behavioral Analysis* (Chicago: Rand McNally, 1964).

17. Charles L. Clapp, *The Congressman: His Work as He Sees It* (New York: Doubleday, 1963), p. 397.

18. Michael J. Malbin, "Of Mountains and Molehills: PACs, Campaigns and Public Policy," in Michael J. Malbin, ed., *Parties, Interest Groups and Campaign Finance Laws* (Washington, D.C.: American Enterprise Institute, 1980), p. 154.

19. Doris A. Graber, *Mass Media and American Politics* (Washington, D.C.: Congressional Quarterly, Inc., 1980), p. 2.

20. Miller and Stokes, "Constituency Influence in Congress," p. 371.

7. Demographic Trends

1. Philip E. Converse, "Change in the American Electorate," in Angus Campbell and Philip E. Converse, eds., *The Human Meaning of Social Change* (New York: Russell Sage Foundation, 1972).

2. Everett Carll Ladd, Jr., and Charles D. Hadley, *Transformations of the American Party System* (New York: Norton, 1975), pp. 15–16.

3. Sorauf, *Party Politics in America*, p. 405.

4. See Warren E. Miller, "Disinterest, Disaffection, and Participation in Presidential Politics," *Political Behavior* 2 (1980): 7–32.

5. Arthur H. Miller and Warren E. Miller, "Rejoinder: Ideology in the 1972 Election," *American Political Science Review* 70 (1976): 832–849.

6. Converse and Markus, "Plus ça change."

7. For data on the changing relationship between age and level of education, see Warren E. Miller, Arthur H. Miller, and Edward J. Schneider, *The American National Election Studies Data Sourcebook, 1952–1978* (Cambridge, Mass.: Harvard University Press, 1980), p. 25.

8. T. W. Adorno et al., *The Authoritarian Personality* (New York: Harper, 1950).

9. Arthur H. Miller and Warren E. Miller, "Partisanship and Performance: 'Rational' Choice in the 1976 Presidential Election" (paper presented at the annual meeting of the American Political Science Association, 1977).

10. Paul Allen Beck, "A Socialization Theory of Partisan Realignment," in Richard G. Niemi, ed., *The Politics of Future Citizens* (San Francisco: Jossey-Bass, 1974).

11. Nie, Verba, and Petrocik, *The Changing American Voter*, p. 68.

8. The Public as an Echo Chamber

1. V. O. Key, *The Responsible Electorate* (Cambridge, Mass.: Harvard University Press, 1966), p. 2.

2. APSA, "Toward a More Responsible Two-Party System: A Report of the Committee on Political Parties, American Political Science Association," *American Political Science Review* 44 (1950): supplement, number 3, part 2.

3. See Evron M. Kirkpatrick, "Toward a More Responsible Party System: Political Science, Policy Science, or Pseudo-Science?" *American Political Science Review* 65 (1971): 965–990.

4. APSA, "Toward a More Responsible Two-Party System," p. 22.

5. Samuel J. Eldersveld, *Political Parties in American Society* (New York: Basic Books, 1982), p. x.

6. APSA, "Toward a More Responsible Two-Party System," p. 95.

7. Ibid., p. 94.

8. Ibid., p. 95.

9. See Paul R. Abramson and John H. Aldrich, "The Decline of Electoral Participation in America," *American Political Science Review* 76 (1982): 502–521.

10. Campbell et al., *The American Voter*, p. 78.

Bibliography

Abramson, Paul R. "Generational Change and the Decline of Party Identification in America: 1952–1974." *American Political Science Review* 70 (1976): 469–478.

Abramson, Paul R., and John H. Aldrich. "The Decline of Electoral Participation in America." *American Political Science Review* 76 (1982): 502–521.

Achen, Christopher H. "Mass Political Attitudes and the Survey Response." *American Political Science Review* 69 (1975): 1218–1231.

Adorno, T. W., Else Frenkel-Brunswik, D. J. Levinson, and R. N. Sanford. *The Authoritarian Personality.* New York: Harper, 1950.

Agranoff, Robert. *The Management of Electoral Campaigns.* Boston: Holbrook Press, Inc., 1976.

American Political Science Association. "Toward a More Responsible Two-Party System: A Report of the Committee on Political Parties." *American Political Science Review* 44 (1950): supplement, number 3, part 2.

Andersen, Kristi. "Generation, Partisan Shift, and Realignment: A Glance Back to the New Deal." In Norman H. Nie, Sidney Verba, and John R. Petrocik, *The Changing American Voter.* Cambridge, Mass.: Harvard University Press, 1976.

Asher, Herbert B. *Presidential Elections and American Politics,* 2d edition. Homewood, Ill.: Dorsey, 1980.

Beck, Paul Allen. "A Socialization Theory of Partisan Realignment." In Richard G. Niemi, ed., *The Politics of Future Citizens.* San Francisco: Jossey-Bass, 1974.

Berelson, Bernard R., Paul F. Lazarfeld, and William N. McPhee. *Voting: A Study of Opinion Formation in a Presidential Campaign.* Chicago: University of Chicago Press, 1954.

Bibby, John F., Thomas E. Mann, and Norman J. Ornstein. *Vital Statistics on Congress, 1980.* Washington, D.C.: American Enterprise Institute, 1980.

Black, Merle, and George B. Rabinowitz. "American Electoral Change: 1952–1972 (with a note on 1976)." In William Crotty, ed., *The Party Symbol: Readings on Political Parties.* San Francisco: W. H. Freeman, 1980.

Boyd, Richard W. "Decline of U.S. Voter Turnout: Structural Explanations." *American Politics Quarterly* 9 (1981): 133–159.

Brady, David W., and Charles S. Bullock III. "Coalition Politics in the House of Representatives." In Lawrence C. Dodd and Bruce I. Oppenheimer, eds., *Congress Reconsidered,* 2d edition. Washington, D.C.: Congressional Quarterly Press, 1981.

Broder, David S. *The Party's Over: The Failure of Politics in America.* New York: Harper and Row, 1971.

Brody, Richard A. "Stability and Change in Party Identification: Presidential to Off-Years." Paper presented at the annual meeting of the American Political Science Association, 1977.

Brody, Richard A., and Benjamin I. Page. "Comment: The Assessment of Policy Voting." *American Political Science Review* 66 (1972): 450–458.

Budge, Ian, Ivor Crewe, and Dennis Fairlie, eds. *Party Identification and Beyond.* New York: Wiley, 1975.

Burnham, Walter Dean. *Critical Elections and the Mainsprings of American Politics.* New York: Norton, 1970.

Caddell, Patrick H. "The Democratic Strategy and Its Electoral

Consequences." In Seymour Martin Lipset, ed., *Party Coalitions in the 1980s*. San Francisco: Institute for Contemporary Studies, 1981.

Campbell, Angus, Gerald Gurin, and Warren E. Miller. *The Voter Decides*. Evanston, Ill.: Row, Peterson and Co., 1954.

Campbell, Angus, Philip E. Converse, Warren E. Miller, and Donald E. Stokes. *The American Voter*. New York: Wiley, 1960.

——— *Elections and the Political Order*. New York: Wiley, 1966.

Clapp, Charles L. *The Congressman: His Work as He Sees It*. New York: Doubleday, 1963.

Converse, Philip E. "The Nature of Belief Systems in Mass Publics." In David E. Apter, ed., *Ideology and Discontent*. Glencoe, Ill.: Free Press, 1964.

——— "The Concept of a Normal Vote." In Angus Campbell et al., *Elections and the Political Order*. New York: Wiley, 1966.

——— "Change in the American Electorate." In Angus Campbell and Philip E. Converse, eds., *The Human Meaning of Social Change*. New York: Russell Sage Foundation, 1972.

——— *The Dynamics of Party Support: Cohort-Analyzing Party Identification*. Beverly Hills, Calif.: Sage Publications, 1976.

Converse, Philip E., and Georges Dupeux. "Politicalization of the Electorate in France and the United States." In Angus Campbell et al., *Elections and the Political Order*. New York: Wiley, 1966.

Converse, Philip E., and Gregory B. Markus. "Plus ça change . . . : The New CPS Election Study Panel." *American Political Science Review* 73 (1979): 32–49.

Cotter, Cornelius, and John F. Bibby. "Institutional Development of Parties and the Thesis of Party Decline." *Political Science Quarterly* 95 (1980): 1–27.

Cronin, Thomas E. *The State of the Presidency*, 2d edition. Boston: Little, Brown and Co., 1980.

Crotty, William J. *Political Reform and the American Experiment*. New York: Crowell, 1977.

Dennis, Jack. "Trends in Public Support for the American Party System." *British Journal of Political Science* 5 (1975): 187–230.

———— "Some Properties of Measures of Partisanship." Paper presented at the annual meeting of the American Political Science Association, 1981.

Downs, Anthony. *An Economic Theory of Democracy.* New York: Harper and Row, 1957.

Eldersveld, Samuel J. "The Independent Vote: Measurement, Characteristics and Implications for Party Strategy." *American Political Science Review* 46 (1952): 732–753.

———— *Political Parties: A Behavioral Analysis.* Chicago: Rand McNally, 1964.

———— *Political Parties in American Society.* New York: Basic Books, 1982.

Farah, Barbara G. "Convention Delegates: Party Reform and the Representativeness of Party Elites, 1972–1980." Paper presented at the annual meeting of the American Political Science Association, 1981.

Ferejohn, John A. "On the Decline of Competition in Congressional Elections." *American Political Science Review* 71 (1977): 166–176.

Finer, S. E. *The Changing British Party System, 1945–1979.* Washington, D.C.: American Enterprise Institute, 1980.

Fiorina, Morris P. *Congress: Keystone of the Washington Establishment.* New Haven: Yale University Press, 1977.

———— "The Decline of Collective Responsibility in American Politics." *Daedalus* 109 (1980): 25–45.

———— *Retrospective Voting in American National Elections.* New Haven, Conn.: Yale University Press, 1981.

Franklin, Charles H., and John E. Jackson. "The Dynamics of Party Identification." Paper presented at the annual meeting of the American Political Science Association, 1981.

Fraser, Donald M. "Democratizing the Democratic Party." In Robert A. Goldwin, ed., *Political Parties in the Eighties.* Washington, D.C.: American Enterprise Institute, 1980.

Graber, Doris A. *Mass Media and American Politics.* Washington, D.C.: Congressional Quarterly, Inc., 1980.

Heclo, Hugh. "The Changing Presidential Office." In Arnold J. Meltsner, ed., *Politics and the Oval Office*. San Francisco: Institute for Contemporary Studies, 1981.

Hofstadter, Richard. *The Idea of a Party System*. Berkeley: University of California Press, 1969.

Jewell, Malcolm E., and David M. Olson. *American State Political Parties and Elections*, rev. ed. Homewood, Ill.: Dorsey, 1982.

Keech, William R., and Donald R. Matthews. *The Party's Choice*. Washington, D.C.: The Brookings Institution, 1976.

Keith, Bruce E., David B. Magleby, Candice J. Nelson, Elizabeth Orr, Mark Westlye, and Raymond E. Wolfinger. "The Myth of the Independent Voter." Paper presented at the annual meeting of the American Political Science Association, 1977.

Key, V. O. *The Responsible Electorate*. Cambridge, Mass.: Harvard University Press, 1966.

Kirkpatrick, Evron. "Toward a More Responsible Party System: Political Science, Policy Science, or Pseudo Science?" *American Political Science Review* 65 (1971): 965–990.

Kirkpatrick, Jeane J. *Dismantling the Parties: Reflections on Party Reform and Party Decomposition*. Washington, D.C.: American Enterprise Institute, 1978.

Ladd, Everett Carll, Jr., and Charles D. Hadley. *Transformations of the American Party System*. New York: Norton, 1975.

Lazarfeld, Paul, Bernard Berelson, and Hazel Gaudet. *The People's Choice*. New York: Columbia University Press, 1944.

Malbin, Michael J. "Of Mountains and Molehills: PACs, Campaigns and Public Policy." In Michael J. Malbin, ed., *Parties, Interest Groups and Campaign Finance Laws*. Washington, D.C.: American Enterprise Institute, 1980.

Mann, Thomas E. *Unsafe at Any Margin*. Washington, D.C.: American Enterprise Institute, 1978.

Mann, Thomas E., and Raymond E. Wolfinger. "Candidates

and Parties in Congressional Elections." *American Political Science Review* 74 (1980): 617–632.

Markus, Gregory B. "The Political Environment and the Dynamics of Public Attitudes: A Panel Study." *American Journal of Political Science* 23 (1979): 338–359.

Markus, Gregory B., and Philip E. Converse. "A Dynamic Simultaneous Model of Electoral Choice." *American Political Science Review* 73 (1979): 1055–70.

Miller, Arthur H. "Normal Vote Analysis: Sensitivity to Change over Time." *American Journal of Political Science* 23 (1979): 406–423.

Miller, Arthur H., and Warren E. Miller. "Rejoinder: Ideology in the 1972 Election." *American Political Science Review* 70 (1976): 832–849.

———— "Partisanship and Performance: 'Rational' Choice in the 1976 Presidential Election." Paper presented at the annual meeting of the American Political Science Association, 1977.

Miller, Arthur H., and Martin P. Wattenberg. "Policy and Performance Voting in the 1980 Election." Paper presented at the annual meeting of the American Political Science Association, 1981.

———— "Measuring Party Identification: Independent or No Partisan Preference?" *American Journal of Political Science* 27 (1983): 106–121.

Miller, Warren E. "The Cross-National Use of Party Identification as a Stimulus to Political Inquiry." In Ian Budge, Ivor Crewe, and Dennis Fairlie, eds., *Party Identification and Beyond.* New York: Wiley, 1976.

———— "Disinterest, Disaffection, and Participation in Presidential Politics." *Political Behavior* 2 (1980): 7–32.

———— "Policy Directions and Presidential Leadership: Alternative Interpretations of the 1980 Presidential Election." Paper presented at the annual meeting of the American Political Science Association, 1981.

Miller, Warren E., and Donald E. Stokes. "Constituency Influence in Congress." In Angus Campbell et al., *Elections and the Political Order*. New York: Wiley, 1966.

Miller, Warren E., and Teresa E. Levitan. *Leadership and Change: The New Politics and the American Electorate*. Cambridge, Mass.: Winthrop, 1976.

Miller, Warren E., Arthur H. Miller, and Edward J. Schneider. *The American National Election Studies Data Sourcebook, 1952–1978*. Cambridge, Mass.: Harvard University Press, 1980.

Nie, Norman H., Sidney Verba, and John R. Petrocik. *The Changing American Voter*. Cambridge, Mass.: Harvard University Press, 1976.

Patterson, Thomas E. *The Mass Media Election: How Americans Choose Their President*. New York: Praeger, 1980.

Petrocik, John R. "An Analysis of the Intransitivities in the Index of Party Identification." *Political Methodology* 1 (1974): 31–47.

Pomper, Gerald. *Voter's Choice: Varieties of American Electoral Behavior*. New York: Dodd, Mead, 1975.

———— "Impacts on the Political System." In Samuel Kirkpatrick, ed., *American Electoral Behavior: Change and Stability*. Beverly Hills, Calif.: Sage Publications, 1976.

Ranney, Austin. *Curing the Mischiefs of Faction: Party Reform in America*. Berkeley: University of California Press, 1975.

———— "The Political Parties: Reform and Decline." In Anthony King, ed., *The New American Political System*. Washington, D.C.: American Enterprise Institute, 1978.

Schattschneider, E. E. *Party Government*. New York: Farrar and Rinehart, 1942.

Seligman, Lester G. "The Presidential Office and the President as Party Leader (with a Postscript on the Kennedy-Nixon Era)." In Jeff Fishel, ed., *Parties and Elections in an Anti-Party Age*. Bloomington: Indiana University Press, 1978.

Shively, W. Phillips. "Information Costs and the Partisan Life Cycle." Paper presented at the annual meeting of the American Political Science Association, 1977.

Sorauf, Frank J. *Party Politics in America,* 4th ed. Boston: Little, Brown and Co., 1980.

Stokes, Donald E., and Warren E. Miller. "Party Government and the Saliency of Congress." *Public Opinion Quarterly* 26 (1962): 531–546.

Sundquist, James L. *Dynamics of the Party System: Alignment and Realignment of Political Parties in the U.S.* Washington, D.C.: The Brookings Institution, 1973.

Tufte, Edward R. "Determinants of the Outcome of Midterm Congressional Elections." *American Political Science Review* 69 (1975): 812–826.

Valentine, David C., and John R. Van Wingen. "Partisanship, Independence, and the Partisan Identification Question." *American Politics Quarterly* 8 (1980): 165–186.

Wattenberg, Martin P. "The Decline of Political Partisanship in the United States: Negativity or Neutrality?" *American Political Science Review* 75 (1981): 941–950.

——— "From Parties to Candidates: Examining the Role of the Media." *Public Opinion Quarterly* 46 (1982): 216–227.

Wattenberg, Martin P., and Arthur H. Miller. "Decay in Regional Party Coalitions: 1952–1980." In Seymour Martin Lipset, ed., *Party Coalitions in the 1980s.* San Francisco: Institute for Contemporary Studies, 1981.

Weisberg, Herbert F. "A Multidimensional Conceptualization of Party Identification." *Political Behavior* 2 (1980): 33–60.

Index